Guaranteeing Performance Improvement

A Purely Practical Positive Approach

Richard F. Gerson, Ph.D.

HRD Press, Inc. • Amherst • Massachusetts

Published by: HRD Press, Inc.
                 22 Amherst Road
                 Amherst, MA 01002
                 800-822-2801 (U.S. and Canada)
                 413-253-3488
                 413-253-3490 (fax)
                 www.hrdpress.com

ISBN 978-1-61014-449-0

Production services by Jean Miller
Editorial services by Sally Farnham
Cover design by Eileen Klockars

Dedication

To my wife, Robbie, and my sons, Michael and Mitchell, who keep me focused on my quest to help everyone achieve and repeat that "perfect performance," and to all my clients and colleagues who have improved their performances through our work together.

Table of Contents

Acknowledgments

It is definitely a cliché to say that no book is ever written solely by the author. And this book is no exception. Let me begin by thanking the thousands of clients and hundreds of thousands of seminar and workshop attendees over the years who allowed me to use the principles and tactics in this book to help them improve their performances. Without their participation in the "live laboratory," nothing in this book would be possible.

I must acknowledge the powerful contribution of my good friend and colleague, Dr. Roger Kaufman. Roger and I have worked together these past several years on various projects, and his strict adherence to scientific rigor has helped me revise my thinking and elevate my performance at work, in my writings, and in my relationships with people. His contribution to this book, as an editor and a friend making helpful suggestions, has been enormous. My only regret is that we did not know each other 30 years ago when we were both at Florida State University. If we did, we could have combined our talents back then and would have already changed the world. Instead, we started a little late, but we are making headway. Roger, thank you from the bottom of my heart for all you've done, do, and will do. I appreciate it more than you know.

A special thank you must go out to various authors and professionals whose work has influenced my own over the years. While I may not have met or worked with some of these people, they have had a positive influence on my work and thought processes. These people include Dr. Martin Seligman (positive psychology); Dr. Mihalyi Csikszentmihalyi (flow); Dr. David Cooperrider (appreciative inquiry); Dr. Bob Singer, Dr. David Pargman, and Dr. Jim Loehr (all sports psychology); Dr. Marcus Buckingham and Dr. Donald Clifton (strengths psychology); and Mauro Panaggio (the head basketball coach at Brockport State College in New York, where I got my Master's degree and began to apply some of these principles with the athletes as his assistant coach).

The International Society for Performance Improvement (ISPI) has been very gracious in publishing many of my articles in their *Performance Improvement Journal (PIJ)* and allowing me to speak on some of the topics in this book at their professional conferences. These platforms have expanded my audience and have therefore enabled more people to become familiar with the "softer side" of performance improvement that I promote. Some of the material in this book is taken from my previously published *PIJ* articles, and I want to thank ISPI for the opportunity to provide the information again.

No book gets to be a book without a great editor and publisher. Bob Carkhuff of HRD Press goes way beyond what anyone will, would, could, or should expect from an editor and publisher. While the book is very good just the way I originally wrote it (if I do say so myself, and I do), the contribution of Bob and his team has made this book infinitely better. Their work with editing the content and creating the design and layout makes me very proud to work with this team. So, to Bob Carkhuff and all of HRD Press, thank you very much.

Finally, I must say thank you again to my wife, Robbie, and my sons, Michael and Mitchell. You three are my life and you know it. You have allowed me time to write this book and all the others, and you provide me with the inspiration to keep on writing. It's your support and love that helps me achieve the high levels of performance in all that I do. My love and appreciation for the three of you will always continue to grow. I guarantee it.

Introduction

Just about everyone wants to get better at what they do. And very few people are totally satisfied with where they are at doing what they are doing at the level they are doing it at. Just think about yourself and people you know. Whatever you have achieved, you probably think or believe there is something more or better out there for you; you just have to figure out how to get there. The science of Human Performance Technology (HPT) and Performance Improvement can guide you from a theoretical perspective. However, most people don't have the time or the inclination to read, understand, and try to apply the theories of the research community. They want an approach to performance improvement that has been tested, will work, and will virtually guarantee them success. Well, two out of three "ain't bad": You can get the first two most of the time, but not the third.

Current approaches to performance improvement in business and in a person's personal life usually focus on a few typical factors. These include competency models covering job descriptions and standards of performance, performance appraisals identifying areas of weakness accompanied by feedback and coaching, some basic skills or remedial training, revisions to an instructional design system, and possibly some work redesign. The problem is that, for all the research and theory that supports their use in controlled or experimental situations, these approaches have had only a minimal positive effect on improving performance in the workplace. One possible reason for this is that people don't readily and accurately apply what is known from the research. This could be one factor in why many performance improvement efforts yield less than stellar results.

The key to successful performance improvement—turning ordinary performers into extraordinary performers—does not lie in the development of the next great competency model, HPT intervention, or instructional design model. It also does not lie in the next great research project or theory of human performance. It rests solely on the shoulders of a human development mastery model. More specifically, it rests within the performer and within a positive approach toward that performer. By this I mean the approach must consider the whole performer, not just the job-related or organizational development competencies, or the system-wide interventions that many people and companies apply. This new approach to performance improvement and human performance technology requires a focus on the psychobehavioral characteristics of the person in addition to their job-related skills.

These include:

- Individual behavioral preferences and tendencies, which are often based on past experiences

- Motivational and emotional styles and tendencies

- Mental tactics related to each performance (before, during, and after the performance)

- Mental and behavioral training techniques

- How they handle and adapt to stress and performance pressure

All the above factors can be assessed and quantified so that the performer always knows exactly where she stands. The old adage *what gets measured gets improved* applies here. After all, measurement is important for improvement. And when a performer knows that her performance will be measured, her motivation to succeed usually increases. Plus, you can develop performance improvement programs that mold intrinsic patterns and preferences to best fit the performer and the job, or you can place the performer in a performance (job, sports, school) situation where she will excel. And, when you combine this approach with the current research-based and proven theoretical models, you get an even more powerful and practical performance improvement program.

But, the success of any performance improvement program must come from within the performer first, including that person's readiness and motivation to perform.

There is another way to help performers reach the top and to guarantee performance improvement in most, if not all, situations. You hear a lot of different phrases such as "Keep your eye on the prize" or "Begin with the end in mind." One that I personally use a great deal is "Results matter." In all cases, there is a focus on what has to be accomplished, and the performer is advised to focus on that objective. We are helped in this regard if we follow the recommendations of Kaufman, who proposes that an Ideal Vision, what he calls Mega, will be the guiding factor in perfect performance.[1] The Ideal Vision describes a world (situation, organization) where everyone is capable and self-reliant, no one controls anyone else, and we appropriately do what we have to do to achieve our shared objectives. The Mega concept is part of Kaufman's Organizational Elements Model, where Mega is the ultimate achievement that benefits society. The other aspects of his model pertain to individuals and organizations to help them achieve perfect performance also.[2]

These approaches can be stretched even further by using techniques borrowed from sports psychology and the mental training of top-level athletes. This requires focus on the overall performance objective and the positives that relate to that performance: strengths, talents, and successes. We can analyze the psychobehavioral and motivational profile and strategies of a top performer, and then develop individualized mental and "physical" training programs to close the gaps between the acknowledged extraordinary performer and the average or ordinary performer. The result is an extremely effective and easy-to-follow way to turn ordinary performers into extraordinary performers.

So we can guarantee performance improvement, not through the use of theoretical models and research, but through performer analysis, performance analysis, and customized psychobehavioral training programs geared to each individual performer. We further guarantee this improvement through a more positive approach to the entire process. And the hidden key is that, with our eye on the prize, this entire approach is a more practical application of proven research.

The Requirement for This Book

There is a definite requirement for this book. A huge gap currently exists in the field between research, theory, and application. Most of the books and articles published in this area focus on the latest research and practice results of a "human performance technology" project, a weakness improvement model, or a training intervention. Other books and articles talk about how to theoretically best apply other models to the performance arena, and you will find several of these in the endnotes for each chapter.

Yet, there are few books that focus on the practical application of performance improvement/enhancement/psychology to the real world, or operational world, where we all live. They give hints on what to do, some talk a little about how to do it, but few focus on a purely practical approach to performance improvement.[3] And, very few of those theoreticians or authors would likely go out on a limb to suggest they can guarantee performance improvement.

A review of articles published by the two leading organizations in this field, the International Society for Performance Improvement (ISPI) and the American Society for Training and Development (ASTD), reveals that they are still primarily research or event based. The articles discuss how someone conducted an experiment to support the use of a model or they talk about the result of an intervention that worked. Some of the articles also talk about the process of an intervention, but the real-world applicability, as compared to the theoretical, is an isolated case.

What the industry (business, people) requires is a practical approach that gets guaranteed results. The question is really very simple, and it is answered by all my clients. When I work with them, what is it that they want and expect from me? **They want RESULTS.**

Do they really care about which theory I use or which approach/process I follow? No, they only care about my helping them achieve results. Do they care if the approach/model I use to help them is research based, statistically validated, and reliably measured? Not really, even though it helps if it is. They only care that what I do for them gets them the results they want and expect in an appropriate time frame. Of course, it helps that all the work is based on proven theory from a variety of fields that has been re-dressed for practical application. That is the purpose of this book. That is what this book will do for you.

This book will equip you with how to develop performer-based improvement programs that generate positive results. Imagine if we can help 1,000 performers improve only 1 percent each month on their jobs (or in sports or school). What will this do for corporate productivity? Imagine if we can help people improve their personal relationships only 1 percent each year. What will this do for someone's personal life? And if both types of improvement occur, how would society benefit from it all?[4]

Think about these benefits. When we know what we have to do and *how* to do it, and the *how* is related to how we normally behave and perform anyway, we will be more motivated to generate the performance improvement. And, when the improvement approach is based on a positive approach to getting better, we will be more inclined to work harder to achieve our desired results. The increased motivation will lead to increased effort on the part of the performer, resulting in the achievement of the desired result. When you take the performer into consideration in all improvement efforts, you can virtually guarantee an improvement will occur, regardless of the specific intervention.[5]

Benefits to the Reader

Here are some of the things readers will benefit from and/or learn by reading this book:

- How to use sports and performance psychology techniques to generate improvements

- Why individual performance patterns are important to performance improvement

- How motivation and performer psychology affect improvement

- How emotional intelligence relates to performance improvement

- Why a focus on the positives leads to performance improvement

- How stress can benefit performance and how stress management leads to performance improvement

Everybody wants to get better at what they do, or at least they should want to get better. The problem is that not everyone knows exactly how to do this—achieve measurable and sustainable performance improvements. This book will guide people and organizations to achieve those desired results by helping them focus on a positive approach to "what makes the performer tick," which then gives everyone the ability to guarantee performance improvement.

Endnotes

1. Roger Kaufman talks extensively on how all that we do, use, and produce must ultimately benefit society, and that anything less is actually thinking too small. He suggests that one of the ways to guarantee performance improvement is to start with the "ultimate end in mind," which he calls the Ideal Vision, or Mega. For more, see his new book, *Change, Choices, and Consequences: A Guide to Mega Thinking and Planning* (Amherst, MA: HRD Press, 2006).

2. Again, Kaufman has written extensively on this concept for close to 40 years now. Others are starting to come around to this Mega concept of thinking and planning. See his book, *Mega Planning* (Thousand Oaks, CA: Sage Publications, 2006). He has also made these concepts available to the general public in another book, *30 Seconds that Can Change Your Life* (Amherst, MA: HRD Press, 2006).

3. In some of my previous books, I took a very practical approach to training the mind to help the body achieve peak performance. The material in that book was also based on research and theory, yet it was made very practical and applicable for the reader. See Gerson, R. F., (2004). *HEADcoaching: Mental training for peak performance.* Bloomington, IN: Authorhouse. Also, see Gerson, R. F., (1998). *Winning the inner game of selling: How sports psychology turns ordinary sales people into extraordinary sales people.* Menlo Park, CA: Crisp. And, Gerson, R. F., (2006). *Achieving high performance: A research-based practical approach.* Amherst, MA: HRD Press.

4. For more on this positive approach to performance improvement and how it can benefit society, read the above-referenced works by Kaufman as well as his articles in the *Performance Improvement Journal* and the *Performance Improvement Quarterly,* which can be accessed at www.ispi.org. Also, see Gerson, R. F., (2006). *Achieving high performance: A research-based practical approach.* Amherst, MA: HRD Press, and Gerson, R. F. & Gerson, R. G., (2006). *Positive performance improvement: A new paradigm to optimize your workforce.* Palo Alto, CA: Davies-Black.

5. I have written about this in several articles that have appeared in the ISPI journal, *Performance Improvement.* You can go to www.ispi.org and search the journal archives under my name for these articles. I have also covered the concept extensively in my book *Achieving High Performance: A Research-Based Practical Approach* (Amherst, MA: HRD Press, 2006).

Chapter 1
Where Have All the Great Ones Gone?

It seems to be getting more and more difficult to find great performers these days. Now, I don't mean the select few, such as Tiger Woods, Michael Jordan, Jack Welch, Luciano Pavarotti, or any other virtuoso. What is missing is a large group of top performers in any field. And the problem seems to stem from an inability to get people to perform at their best for a sustained period of time. They say if you read 10 books on one subject over the course of a year, you will know more about that subject than 95 percent of the people in the world. You will be considered an expert. Also, we are often told that if we practice a single skill on a regular basis for 10 years, we can become or at least be considered world class. Of course, we'll have to earn that title through our performances. In any case, there are not enough top performers around, and we've all got to wonder why.

Meet Larry. Larry was a starting guard on a major college basketball team during his sophomore and junior years. The team was going to look to him for leadership in his senior season as well as put the burden of winning squarely on his shoulders. Larry was a good ball handler, a better than average outside shooter, and he played decent defense. He appeared to have an all-around game. Yet, he could barely make 50 percent of his foul shots. Imagine a top performer being unable to make more than half his free throws. No one guarding him. No hand in his face. No "pressure" from the clock. And he still couldn't get the job done.

So the coach brought in a shooting coach, thinking it was a mechanics problem. The shooting coach made a few changes and Larry practiced diligently while the shooting coach was on the court. But, during games, he still had the same problems at the foul line. Your starting senior guard can't shoot a foul shot and he has to be in the game. This could have been very costly for the team at the end of a close game. Since the mechanical solutions were not working, the head coach looked for other answers. That's when I started working with Larry.

Larry's problem was not in his mechanics. It was in what golfers call "swing thoughts." These are the thoughts that run through a golfer's mind just before he or she swings the club. More often than not, these thoughts are negative: "You're so terrible" or "You can't play this game—why are you even trying?" Other negative thoughts are "Don't do anything wrong" and the athlete eventually listens and screws up by doing the exact thing he or she wasn't supposed to do. Larry's "shooting thoughts" were "Everyone's watching me—now what?" and "If I don't make it, I'll let everyone down." Larry was putting undue pressure on himself and that was causing his poor foul shooting. Since he was motivated to be successful, we worked on his shooting thoughts, his self-esteem, and his belief system about his abilities as a basketball player. In a couple of weeks, he was shooting 70 percent from the foul line.

Engaging the Performer

When people engage in a performance, they bring to it a mindset; a set of behaviors, beliefs, and values; and a heart full of emotions. We must influence all of these factors in order to guarantee and achieve performance improvements. It does not matter how good our theories, techniques, and technologies are if we forget about the people "doing" the performance. And we must also include the performer's psychological approach to taking action. We must consider their levels of self-confidence and self-esteem, how they deal with performance anxiety, how well they perform under pressure, if they set goals, their expectations of success, their intrinsic reward system, and what motivates them to achieve. We must focus heavily on the psychology of performance improvement if we really want to upgrade people's performances and get them truly interested in being the best they can be.

This idea is really not so new, as it was suggested to us decades ago in the field of psychology that in order to improve performance, we must treat individuals in such a way that we account for their intrinsic motivations, belief and behavior systems, and their perceptions of the impact of their performances. This tells me that we must pay attention to the psychology of performance improvement in order to get real change, attain higher levels of performance, and eventually, be able to guarantee performance improvement.

There is only one way to guarantee performance improvement and to make sure individuals move from ordinary performance to extraordinary performance. To do this, we must place our focus squarely on the "object of our affections"—the performer. We must spend more time with the human portion of the human performance technology equation. After all, what good is all the science of human performance technology if the performer:

1.   Does not want us to know why he does what he does?

2.   Does not see the meaningfulness and relevance of achieving high performance?

3.   Does not want to share all the information he has acquired about and from previous performances?

4.   Wants to totally control all aspects of the performance?

5.   Wants to stay at the level he is already at and has no desire to improve or elevate his performance?

That is why we must focus on the performer and what he wants. Here are some things we must consider to get the performer more involved with the performance improvement effort:

- Memories
- Emotions
- Motivations
- Experiences
- Belief systems
- Self-esteem
- Confidence
- Reinforcers
- Perceived pain of changing or not changing
- Thoughts

This list is not totally inclusive, but it is comprehensive enough to give you an idea of all that goes into a person's decision about improving performance as well as what might be going through that person's mind. No matter what we do to help, if the person decides she doesn't want our help, we will not get that improved performance. So getting the person engaged in the performance improvement effort is one of the first steps toward guaranteeing performance improvement.

The Mindset of the Performer

Every performer enters each performance situation in a specific mindset or mental state. Some are positive, some are neutral, some are negative, and some just don't have a clue. Their mental state definitely affects how well they perform and the level they perform at. People who are self-confident and believe in their abilities do well in most situations more often than those who are not self-confident or doubt their abilities. This is because each successful performance increases their feelings of competence, confidence, and self-worth. Plus, each successful performance is self-reinforcing, which motivates the person to want to engage in that same or a similar performance again in order to achieve similar results.

A positive attitude and a high level of self-esteem are essential to superior performances.[1] A performer who has already experienced success in previous activities will enter into future performance situations with an expectation for future success. High perceived expectations of success result in significant performance improvements over previous efforts as well as higher levels of achievement on repetitive tasks. When you combine these factors with a task that is matched to the performer's abilities and that is inherently challenging, the performer quite often enters into a flow state[2] (or "zone") that produces a peak performance.[3]

It is up to us as performance technologists to take these factors into account as they affect the performer's mental state. We must consider their self-esteem, their expectations for success, how they perceive the task in relation to their current skill set, and how well they have done on previous related tasks. One way we can ensure that we help performers achieve a positive mental state is to verbally praise and reinforce both their successful behaviors and their successful approximations of the desired behaviors so that these behaviors will be repeated and the intrinsic motivation of the performers will increase.[4]

Another aspect of the performer's mental state that we must consider is how this person responds to and performs under stress. Stress and adversity have a major effect on performance improvements and results. However, they are not really the culprits that cause a performance decrement or an inability to learn. It is the performer's reaction to stress, adversity, and anxiety that determines the level of improvement as well as the result. We must teach people how to relax and perform under pressure if we want to realize high-level performance results.

Mastering the Psychology of Performance Improvement

We can all accept the fact that the mind plays an important part in everything we do. Given that this is the case, why do we spend so much time on systems, technology, and media when we try to improve performance, instead of spending time on the individual performer? Pouring information into performers does not guarantee that they will respond in a positive manner to our improvement overtures. In fact, there is a better possibility that they will not respond because most people don't like to be told what to do.

The performer must see performance improvement as something that is intrinsically rewarding. The performer must receive self-satisfaction from getting better at whatever he or she is doing. In this way, the performer will remain intrinsically motivated and will want to repeat the task again and again. While there are times when extrinsic rewards can also help improve performance, the continued provision of extrinsic or external rewards (such as money, prizes, etc.) every time a performer approximates an improvement or achieves a performance goal will probably cause a loss of intrinsic motivation for that task.[5]

There are many authors who promote the behaviorist approach to performance improvement.[6] For them, every time someone does something right, you give them a reward or positive reinforcement. Then that person will be "motivated" to repeat the behavior under the premise that what gets rewarded gets repeated.

This is only true in certain situations and for only a short period of time. Actually, it works more often for pigeons and rats in a maze than it does for people. If the performer does not believe he or she is gaining from the performance, either psychologically, emotionally, or physically, then that "desired behavior" will not be repeated, regardless of the reward or reinforcement. What the behaviorist approach appears to leave out is the cognition of the performer, even though the more recent models do talk about the role of the person (organism). We must remember that every person thinks (or should think) about what he or she is doing, either consciously or subconsciously. And those thoughts lead to emotions that become attached to the performance. Sometimes, the emotions come before the thoughts, but the attachment still occurs. This is why we must pay attention to both the mental state and the emotions of the performer when we are trying to bring about performance improvement.[7]

Another area where we are remiss as human performance technologists is that we either negate or forget about the roles commitment, desire, and passion play in performance improvement. Yes, these are types of emotions, and yes, they do have an effect on performance. But we must remember that all learning, memory recall, and performance occur best when the current situation approximates the previous performance situation. This means that not only must the environment be similar, the emotional state of the performer must be similar.[8]

If we are highly aroused when we learn a new way to perform an old task, or even when we learn a new task, then we should also be highly aroused when we are expected to perform that task in a different situation. If we have a passion for doing something, we must exhibit that passion every time if we want to achieve a high level of performance. Conversely, when we are not committed or passionate about something, we either do not do it at all or we just go through the motions without the necessary emotions.

How many times have you done everything exactly according to the Human Performance Technology (HPT) Model? You completed your front end analysis, identified your performance gaps, identified and developed the appropriate intervention, created the proper performance aids that would lead to performance improvement, implemented the intervention, and then watched it fall flat on its face? What was missing? What was missing was the analysis of the performer, such as his emotions, thoughts, motives, decisions, and feelings. Along with that is the guarantee to the performer that you would help him improve.

Have you ever wondered why it is so difficult to guarantee performance improvement? You would think that with all the theories, technologies, and models we have in the field that we would be the first ones to jump up and say we can guarantee improvement. Yet, very few, if any, performance consultants are willing to stick their necks out and tell a client they will definitely help them improve performance. It makes you wonder, doesn't it? If we are so good at what we do, why won't we guarantee our work? Here are a few possible reasons.

Problems in Performance Improvement

Once you've identified that a true gap in performance exists, and you determine the appropriate intervention, what are some things that can derail the effort? There are four issues that must be considered, aside from the internal workings of the actual performer. These are a lack of clear goals, objectives, and performance expectations; a lack of proper measurement tools; a poor performer/task fit; and an inappropriate reward system for performance-related behaviors. Let's look at them individually.

Lack of Clear Goals, Objectives, and Expectations. It is imperative that the performer know what is expected of him. Goals and objectives must be properly established, agreed upon, and then linked to performance expectations so that the performer knows where she starts and where she is expected to end up. When you establish these goals and objectives, you are not determining the process by which the person will perform or achieve the new goals. You are simply stating, in measurable terms, what the final performance will accomplish, look like, or produce. Then you and the performer must totally agree on these goals and objectives so that the actual expectations can be established. Once this is all done, and the performer buys in to the whole concept, you have a good chance of seeing performance improvement. Performer buy-in also increases that person's motivation to perform well. So get clear on your goals, objectives, and expectations, ensure performer agreement and buy-in, and make certain that both you and the performer are aligned with what the final accomplishment will look like.

Lack of Proper Measurement Tools. The old adage *What gets measured gets improved* is crucial if you want to guarantee performance improvement. People simply perform better when they know they are being measured (some say "watched"). And that is not necessarily bad. You can have what they call the Hawthorne Effect, where changing the work environment leads to increases in performance, or the Social Facilitation Effect, where performing in front of somebody (or a crowd) leads to an increase in performance. In any case, the perception of observational and subjective measurement on the part of the performer usually is sufficient to lead to performance improvement.

You also have to establish appropriate objective measures. Whatever the units of measurement are or are going to be, you must make certain that you and the performer agree on them, fully understand them, and know how they relate to the actual performance. For example, if you are going to work with someone to improve their foul shooting in basketball, and you've established certain measurements for assessing and evaluating technique, then you will focus on the shooting technique. In reality, it is not the technique that is so important. It is whether or not the ball goes in. So the measurement should actually be successful foul shots, not perfect technique (although better technique might help a person make more foul shots).

This is a problem we run into all the time in performance improvement work. We spend so much time identifying and determining the processes we will use that we feel compelled to measure them. Process measurements are fine, if you want to eventually improve processes. But they are not the measurements that should be used if you want to improve performance. Appropriate measures for performance include units sold, shots made, weight lost, scrap reduced, customer repurchases, and the list goes on. You can easily see that these measures relate to end results (I am using the term *results* here in a slightly different manner than Kaufman and his multi-level delineation of the term *results*), and end results are the only thing that matter when you want performance improvement.

Poor Performer/Task Fit. This is a guaranteed recipe for performance failure. Too often, when we have a task to be completed, we involve people whose strengths do not fit well with that task. We ask them to do things they are not well-suited for or are totally incapable of accomplishing at a high level. Yet, for some strange reason, we still believe that if we ask "hard" enough, cajole long enough, and train often enough, we will get them to perform well. You can't get a sprinter to win a marathon. You can't get a top field sales representative to handle accounting tasks the same way a CPA would handle them. And you can't expect anyone to perform well if they are not given the tools for the task at hand.

This particular problem should also be expanded to include the performance environment. If you put a good performer in a bad system, the system will win most of the time. What this means is that the poor performance environment, the lack of tools or resources, or the inability of the system to support the performer or the performance will lead to a less than stellar result. While a good or great system can somehow elevate the performance of a poor performer, a bad system will definitely pull down the performance of a great performer. This holds true for both physical and mental tasks.

How can you expect a student who is not good at math to excel in a classroom of advanced math students? You can't. The knowledge isn't there and the cognitive strain that would be put on the student is enormous. Tutoring (training) won't help that much, if at all. The child is simply not ready to perform at the required level because she does not have the mental skills necessary to do the work. Similarly, how can you expect a brain surgeon to possess the same knowledge as an electrical engineer and to perform in the engineer's environment at the same level as the electrical engineer? You can't. The mental skills are totally different, even though there may be some similarity between the physical skills of finger manipulation, dexterity, and fine motor movements.

Previous works by Gerson and Gerson and the Gallup Organization[9] have stressed the importance of playing to the performer's strengths. This makes the task easier to perform, a positive result is virtually assured, and the performer steadily builds confidence and is willing to take on the task again as well as additional, and possibly more difficult or complex, tasks. Playing to someone's strengths makes that person feel good about themselves, about what they are doing, and what they will do next. A strengths orientation enhances the performer/ task fit, makes the performer truly believe that "I can do that," and gets the person and the organization the result they want to achieve.

Inappropriate Rewards. Here is where we get into trouble when we want to improve performance. Too many people think that if you simply provide rewards, performance will improve. Give people more money for what they do and their next performance will be at a higher level. Give people movie passes or gift cards to a restaurant and they will "blow the doors" off their next performance. Tell salespeople they will win a car or a vacation trip and you can just about guarantee that everyone's sales will go up. The problem is that these beliefs are all wrong.

Money doesn't motivate everyone. The science of behavioral economics tells us that when people have enough money to satisfy their basic requirements in life, more money does not necessarily make them happier or more satisfied. Just look at how many lottery winners are now broke, have gotten divorced, and have even committed suicide. Also, take a look at the baby boomer marketplace. Many of these people are already financially secure, so giving them money to improve or sustain or repeat a performance can have little or no effect. Money may be an integral part of someone's life, but it does not guarantee future performance improvement.

The other problem with the current thinking on rewards for performance is that the same reward or reinforcement approach works for everyone. That is a huge mistake. Different people are reinforced through different things. Some may want money, some may want food, some may want time off, some may want verbal reinforcement, and some may want physical contact. I remember when my oldest son was 10 years old and he did something very well. I *told* him what a great job he did and that Daddy was giving him a pat on the back. He said to me that I never gave him a pat on the back, all I did was tell him when he did well. I asked him if he wanted me to physically pat him on the back and he said yes, that would make him feel very good and very proud. So, I literally patted him on the back from then on when I wanted to compliment him on a job well done. My youngest son, when he was the same age, was satisfied with the verbal reinforcement for a job well done. Different strokes for different folks.

Here is a recommendation that is so simple, I don't know why everyone does not implement it. When I have shared it with small to mid-size companies, they instantly see the wisdom in it and get right to it. When I shared it with large companies, some immediately got on board while others saw the task as overwhelming because of the number of employees in the company. Here is the advice: Just go out and ask each employee exactly what they want as a reward or reinforcement, and then make sure each manager, department head, and supervisor knows the individual "motivator" for each employee. Yes, this will take some time with large numbers of employees. And yes, it will take more time to put the information into some sort of database. But the result will be more than worth it because now each employee will receive the reward or reinforcement that is personalized for them. This will increase their buy-in to future tasks, their motivation to repeat the task at a high level, and their willingness to perform even if the odds seem to be against them. A little personalized positive reinforcement will generate a lot of high-level positive results.

Endnotes

1. This relationship is a foundation of the positive psychology movement. Much of the work in the area of optimism and high performance was pioneered by Martin Seligman, who coined the terms *learned helplessness* and *learned optimism.* His research supports the relationship among attitudes, beliefs, and performance. His book, *Authentic Happiness* (New York: Free Press, 2002) covers this in great detail.

2. The concept of flow was introduced by M. Csikszentmihalyi in the book *Flow.* (New York: Harper, 1990) and studied experimentally by him and others using athletes, artists, dancers, and teachers, to name a few professions. Now, the terms *flow* and *flow state* (or *state of flow*) are part of everyday language.

3. See Gerson, R. F., (2004). *HEADcoaching: Mental training for peak performance.* Bloomington, IN: Authorhouse.

4. You will find information on this relationship and how these factors affect confidence and future successful performances in R. M. Kanter's book *Confidence* (New York: Crown Business, 2004). You will also find similar information in A. Daniels's book *Bringing Out the Best in People* (New York: McGraw-Hill, 2000). You will find a comprehensive summary of work on intrinsic and extrinsic motivation as it relates to performance in the book by E.

Deci and R. Ryan, *The Handbook of Self-Determination Research* (New York: University of Rochester Press, 2005).

5.   See Kohn, A., (1999). *Punished by rewards*. Boston: Mariner Books.

6.   Look at A. Daniels's book *Bringing Out the Best in People* (New York: McGraw-Hill, 2000) as one accepted example of this approach, as well as his other books on how to use behaviorism to manage and improve performance.

7.   You can find more information on this in the book by R. F. Gerson, *Achieving High Performance: A Research-based Practical Approach* (Amherst, MA: HRD Press, 2006).

8.   There is more information on this concept in the Gerson HEADcoaching reference (Note 3) as well as the Kanter book on confidence (Note 4).

9.   See Gerson, R. F., & Gerson, R. G., (2006). *Positive performance improvement: A new paradigm for optimizing your workforce*. Palo Alto, CA: Davies-Black. Also spend some time with books by the Gallup organization, including *First, Break All the Rules*, by M. Buckingham & C. Coffman (New York: Simon & Schuster, 1999) and *The One Thing You Need to Know*, by M. Buckingham (New York: Free Press, 2005).

Chapter 2
It's the People, Stupid

Okay, here's the situation: You've already completed your needs assessment, analyzed your gaps in performance, selected your intervention, and now you're ready to present your plan to the decision makers. You get your data together, create a knock-out slide presentation, and develop your FAQ sheet. You're ready, and you go in there and knock their socks off—at least in your mind. You do a great job, you feel great about your presentation, and all you're waiting for is the approval to go ahead with the project. After all, how could they not approve the project? You've given them the process you will use to improve performance, the potential return on investment, and what they can expect if the intervention works. And then someone asks you, "Can you *guarantee* this will work?" And you sit (or stand) there stunned, your mouth drops open, and you start groping for words.

Guarantee it will work? What are they thinking? Of course, you can't *guarantee* anything will work. You have to give it your best shot and then hope for the best. But, in reality, you know hope is not a strategy (nor is it a tactic). So what do you do? Your mind races as you think of the past programs that were implemented in the company: TQM, re-engineering, six sigma, and the list goes on. While these programs worked to some degree, none of them ever truly lived up to their billing. So since these previous organization-wide initiatives did not get all the results they promised, how are you supposed to *guarantee* the results from your intervention?

And what do they expect from you? You've provided the information on the theory behind your assessment and selection of the intervention, you've supported the process you will use with previous research results, and you even tried to talk to them about money in a way they would understand— ROI. Now someone wants you to guarantee your work!? What are they, crazy?

Yes, they are crazy like a fox. Why shouldn't we, as performance consultants (both internal and external), be able to guarantee our work? Why shouldn't we stand up there and say, that *yes,* without a doubt, this will work. It will work for the individual performer, it will work on the group or team level, it will work for the organization, and ultimately, it will work for society." The problem is that we, the performance improvement professionals, really don't have the confidence to say that what we do will always work. The reason is that we spend too much time on the theory, research, and technology instead of spending the time where we should. We do a great job of analyzing performance problems and proposing workable solutions. We also do an excellent job of implementing those solutions when we are given the chance. Therefore, if we are so good, why is it so difficult for us to get the results that people want to see with regards to performance improvement?

People, People Who Need People (with apologies to the song)

The reason is that our theories, models, and assumptions are technically sound, but they are not very people oriented. In fact, they seem to be very sterile, and they proceed in a lock-step manner. It is almost as if you should follow the boxes and lines in a model, and the desired performance will come out at the other end. We all know that this does not happen as often as it should. It is extremely important for us as a field of inquiry to take into account both the people side of performance improvement and the emotional side of it. We have to engage both the hearts and minds of the performers if we are ever going to get transferable results and lasting improvements. Unfortunately, the current theories and techniques seem to forget about this important aspect of performance improvement.

When people (or a group, organization, or society) engage in a performance, they bring to it a mindset; a set of behaviors, beliefs, and values; and a heart full of emotions. We must account for and influence all of these factors in order to achieve and guarantee performance improvements. It does not matter how good our theories and technologies are if we forget about the people "doing" the performance and the other people they are doing the performance with. Now before someone gets into a debate about how some people perform independently, I will agree with that statement, to a point. While someone may do a task independently, they never perform in a vacuum. Everything they do will have an effect on someone else or some other group within a system. So we have to account for both the individual performer and the other people who will either be involved with the performance or affected by the performance.

Some of the things we have to look at with respect to the individual performer include their psychological approach to taking action, their levels of self-confidence and self-esteem, how they deal with performance anxiety, how well they perform under pressure, if they set goals and objectives, their expectations of success, their intrinsic reward system, what external reinforcements they desire, and what motivates them to achieve. We must focus on the psychology of performance improvement if we really want to upgrade people's performances and guarantee their improvement. We must pay attention to the psychology of the performer in order to get real change and guarantee performance improvement.

The Mental State of the Performer

Every performer enters each performance situation in a specific mental state. Their mental state definitely affects how well they perform and if they achieve their performance results. Performers who are self-confident and believe in their abilities do well on tasks more often than those who are not self-confident or doubt their abilities. This is because each successful performance increases their feelings of competence, confidence, and self-worth.

A positive attitude and a high level of self-esteem are essential to superior performances. A performer who has already experienced success in previous activities will enter into future performance situations with an expectation for future success. High perceived expectations of success result in significant performance improvements over previous efforts as well as higher levels of achievement on repetitive tasks. When you combine these factors with a task that is matched to the performer's abilities and is inherently challenging, you are playing to that person's strengths and increasing the possibility that she will enter into a flow state that produces a peak performance. This is also the basis for the positive psychology and strengths psychology approach to enhanced performance: Match the task to the strengths, reinforce the results, and repeat.[1] The reason they will be repeated is because everyone feels good when someone else tells them how well they did. This satisfies the most important emotional requirement of a person: to be and feel appreciated.[2]

The performer must receive self-satisfaction from getting better at whatever he or she is doing. In this way, the performer will remain intrinsically motivated and will want to repeat the task again and again. Another area where we are remiss as human performance technologists is that we either negate or forget about the roles that commitment, desire, and passion play in performance improvement. Yes, these are types of emotions, and yes, they do have an effect on performance. But we must remember that all learning, memory recall, and performance occur best when the current situation approximates the previous performance situation. This means that not only must the environment be similar, the emotional state of the performer must be similar.[3]

If we are highly aroused when we learn a new way to perform an old task (performance improvement), or even when we learn a new task, then we must also be (or should be) highly aroused when we are expected to perform that task in a different real-world situation. If we have a passion for doing something, we must exhibit that passion every time if we want to achieve a high level of performance. Conversely, when we are not committed or passionate about something, we either do not do it at all or we just go through the motions without the necessary emotions. We have to spend more time on the people side of the HPT model. When you do this, you will master the psychology of performance improvement and come closer to being able to guarantee your results.

Seven Rs Guarantee Performance Improvement

I have found that the following seven actions or activities usually lead to performance improvement: rapport, respect, response, reinforcement, repetition, rhythm, and ritual. First, you must establish **rapport** with the performer. Whether you are a coach, manager, or co-worker, the performer must know that you are on the same team with regards to this improvement effort. The performer must feel comfortable with you and the task at hand in order to effectively and successfully engage in performance improvement.

The next thing you must do is **respect** the performer and communicate that respect. Respect is shown in many ways. You must acknowledge the performer's efforts. You must communicate that you appreciate those efforts. And you must be willing to allow the performer to learn from mistakes.

Following this, you must demonstrate as well as clearly explain the desired **response** or response set. The performer must know exactly what must be done, how it looks when it is done correctly, and how it feels when it is right. When the performer does it right, you must **reinforce** the performance. Verbal feedback and praise is usually sufficient at this point in time. This recognition is more psychological and therefore longer lasting than tokens or financial incentives. The positive reinforcement will also lead to a **repetition** of the appropriate response (improvement). The more the performer repeats the proper response, the more it becomes ingrained in memory so that future performances can occur at a high level, as if automatically.

If you can create a **rhythm** to the performance, it will be easier for the performer. Everything has a rhythm to it and you must help the performer identify the best rhythm associated with the improvement task. Pay attention to the way the performer moves, what he or she says (often this is an outward display of thought processes), and what he or she does when the performance is completed. Rhythm helps people do whatever they do better.

Then sit back and watch the types of **rituals** the performer creates to complete the new skill. Basketball players bounce the ball several times before shooting a foul shot. Golfers move the club back and forth before hitting the ball. Dancers use a certain stretching routine before they perform. These are all rituals. When a performer develops a ritual for a task, then you can be sure there will be improvement as well as a continued high level of achievement.

There you have it. A simple yet effective way to improve performance, guaranteed. Start and end with the person. Focus on the psychological issues related to performance improvement instead of the technological issues. Pay attention to motives, beliefs, values, attributions, the ability to perform under stress, performance rituals, affirmations, expectations of success, and the emotional state of the performer. While this may seem like a great deal to focus on, you really cannot avoid it. Most performance improvement efforts that focus on the technology of the field do not always achieve the desired results. Only by focusing on the person first, and the psychology of that person in particular, will you achieve continual performance improvement. And if you really want to guarantee that improvement over time, you must focus on the emotions of the performer.

Now that we've covered the psychology of the performer, let's take a look at the performer herself. It's what I call the people side of guaranteeing performance improvement.

The People Side of Performance Improvement

When you consider the people side of performance improvement and look at the person as a performance system that you must optimize, you get the results you are looking for, and then some. In fact, you are able to virtually guarantee that performance improvement will occur. Here are 11 keys that will open the doors for performance improvement. While they are written to you and for you as the first person reader, you can also apply them to people you work with, live with, and socialize with to get the performance improvements you desire.

Key Number 1: Positive Attitude. You must have a positive attitude toward everything you do and everyone you meet. You must start with yourself. You have to have a good attitude toward yourself. You must say positive things to yourself every day (affirmations). You must talk to yourself in a positive manner (positive self-talk). You must know that you are responsible for all the results of your behaviors (accomplishments and attributions). And you must believe that everything you do, use, and produce will be for the benefit and general good of all people, organizations, and society.[4] Think positively, and your performance will improve most of the time. Plus, you will open many other doors to success.

Key Number 2: High Self-esteem/Positive Self-image. What you think of yourself speaks volumes about who you are and how people respond to you. A high self-esteem establishes a positive achievement cycle in your life. Your positive self-image attracts other people to you like a powerful magnet. These people want to be around you, and either consciously or intuitively, they want to help you succeed. Because of all this, your performance improves.

You build a high level of self-esteem through your positive attitude and by having confidence in yourself as a person. Believe that you can do anything you set your mind to doing. You can achieve any level of performance that you make up your mind to achieve, within reason. Measure your self-worth according to your own standards, not those set for you by other people.

So keep your self-image and self-esteem high. Do things that feel good and right for you. If you want other people to compliment you, compliment them first. If you want other people to make you feel good, which will build your self-esteem, do something to make other people feel good first. You can always be successful at building your own self-esteem if you help others build theirs first. And you can always improve your performance by helping other people improve theirs first. Then you both feel good.

Key Number 3: Communication Skills. Successful people are great communicators. They are able to convince, influence, persuade, and communicate their ideas, dreams, and goals to other people, and enlist their aid to achieve those goals. Also, successful people are excellent listeners. In fact, if you ever want to be remembered as a great conversationalist, just listen.

Effective communication is only effective based on the response you get. If you do not get the other person to understand or respond the way you meant them to, then you have not been effective as a communicator. This is one of the main causes for people not accomplishing what they set out to do. They just do not understand the task at hand, what is expected of them, or how they should go about performing. Or you do not make yourself clear to other people about what you expect regarding their performance.

Communication is also the key to success in all interpersonal relationships, and it is a foundational element of the people side of performance improvement. How do you get to be an effective communicator so that you can help people improve their performance? You learn about the other person. Learn their speaking style, the words they use, and the results they are looking for when they communicate. Then feed this back to them by flexing your style and you will see a magnificent change occur as the two of you develop complete rapport (which is one of the seven Rs from the previous section that can guarantee performance improvement). Complete rapport places you at the point that you think you know what the other person is saying before they say it.

Key Number 4: Lifelong Learning. Successful people and organizations are constantly learning. They read, go to seminars, watch specific programs on television, listen to tapes, and do everything possible to learn whatever they can about their area of endeavor as well as other areas. Not only that, they enjoy being mentors and coaches to other people who are motivated to learn for life. So regardless of where you stopped your formal education, now is the time to start learning again. The more you learn, the more you improve.

Key Number 5: Love. You have to love yourself before you can love others. The more love you give, the more you will get back in return. At work, consider showing you care about other people. We are not talking about romantic love here. Just good old-fashioned caring, concern, and understanding. When people know you care about them, they do whatever they can to please you and make you happy. If you are their manager, they will evidence this by upgrading their skills and improving their performances. For a small effort on your part, you can get a tremendous return on your investment. And remember, you can never give more love to someone else than you are capable of giving yourself or receiving from someone else.

Key Number 6: Health and Well-being. Take care of yourself: Eat right, think right, and exercise. Relax often and get enough sleep. When you look and feel good, the world seems to be a better place. People who are healthy and well simply perform better. They have more energy, more stamina, and they can deal more effectively with stress.

Most performance improvement issues or problems have a stress component related to them. People under too much stress, or too little for that matter, do not perform as well as they should. In fact, performance suffers significantly in most cases. However, when you are well, you can manage your stress better plus handle performance pressures better, which enables you to perform at a higher level.[5]

Key Number 7: Motivation. The door to successful performance improvement opens wide for you when you are intrinsically motivated. That means your desires and your satisfaction from performance come from within, not from some external reward source.

You must also determine your level of achievement motivation. What is it you truly want to achieve, and how much are you willing to risk getting it? Do you want to be involved in tasks that are so simple anyone can achieve them? Or do you want to be involved with accomplishing something with a moderate to high degree of difficulty? Your answers to these questions will identify your achievement motivation related to your performances.

Another aspect of motivation involves the direction of your motivation. Do you move toward a goal or away from it? Do you have a fear of success or a fear of failure? Are you willing to put more effort into achieving pleasure, or will avoiding some sort of pain motivate you to action? These are real factors in determining how well you use this key to success, so you must know what causes you to act, how you interpret your actions, and what you plan to do about similar situations next time.

Here is one more thing that makes this key work effectively. You must develop your own reward systems. When you determine the rewards for your performances, you stay intrinsically motivated. If you establish many external rewards, or let your company establish the rewards for you without your involvement, you will find your motivation and your associated performance levels lessening over time. That's because you really don't "own the rewards." So make sure you know exactly what you want when you succeed and how you will reinforce and reward yourself.

Key Number 8: Goal and Objectives Setting. This is closely aligned with motivation. Most people never set goals or specify measurable performance objectives. Of those who do, only 3 to 5 percent actually write down their goals. It is this small percentage of people who have a purpose in life to which they can be committed.

You must write down your goals for performance improvement and be very specific about the objective results you are trying to achieve. What will goal attainment or success look, sound, and feel like? What are the objective measurements that will let you know your performance has improved? How will you know you have gotten the exact result you wanted? And what changes in behavior will be evident so that you will know your goal has been reached?

Make all your goal statements personal, measurable, and set within a reasonable time frame, and make sure they are results-oriented. Action-oriented behaviors are no longer enough to guarantee goal attainment and success. These are statements about what you are going to do, but they often leave out what you are going to accomplish. You have got to have results-oriented behaviors so that you will know exactly when you've achieved your objective. Also, you must take into account the emotional component of performance, achievement, and improvement. Then you will be committed to doing whatever it takes to stay focused on your purpose and achieve your goals and objectives repeatedly.

Key Number 9: Relaxation. Relaxation is a key that also benefits all the other keys. Relaxation helps you visualize your way to successful performance improvement, manage stress, engage in positive self-talk, build and rebuild your self-image, and train your mind and body for peak performances. You must engage in some form of relaxation every day.

The other benefit to relaxation is that all—and I mean all—peak performances and major improvements come when your mind and body are in a state of relaxed alertness. You are ready to perform at your peak and you are willing to let your mind and body work together without conscious intervention. This is the state of flow where all your body and brain systems work together perfectly. It is that desired "place" that everyone tries to achieve. When you are in a state of flow, or in the zone as some people call it, you do not have to try so hard to achieve. In fact, you feel like you are not even trying at all. Successful performances just happen. So relax, enter flow, achieve, and improve.

Key Number 10: Visualization. Visualization is the process of imagining yourself being successful. Since the mind does not know the difference between a real or an imagined event, when you picture yourself improving and being successful, your mind will believe it as fact. Then it does everything in its power to make that image a reality.

Visualization is a skill that can be developed and nurtured. It can be used to erase bad performances from the past and to develop future positive behaviors. When you combine visualization with relaxation and goal setting, you establish a pattern

that leads to continual self-improvement, successful performance improvement, and achievement.

Key Number 11. Personal Value System. This may be the
most important key to performance improvement and your ultimate success. Without a value system, you will not be able to
make decisions, define your true purpose in life, and carry out
the behaviors necessary to achieve your objectives.

Values are the foundation for all you do. Your decisions
and behavioral choices are based on your value system. Whom
you associate with and relate to are based on your values.
When your behaviors are incongruent with your values, you
feel tremendous discomfort. You no longer function optimally,
either psychologically or physically. The result is a poor performance, a deteriorating relationship, or a negative attitude
toward yourself. Identify your values, clarify them, and understand how they relate to your performance. Then you will see
tremendous performance improvements as your value system
guides your achievement behaviors.

There are your 11 keys to the people side of performance
improvement. You will notice that nothing was said about job
aids, the work environment, training, cross training, retraining,
job redesign, systems approaches, or any of the other "standard" approaches to performance improvement. These 11 keys
are the true foundation of **human** performance technology.
Employers, companies, and individuals that begin to focus on
the performer first, and the characteristics of the performer that
make him or her unique, will realize significant performance
improvements on a regular basis.

It's the People, Smarty

If your performance improvement efforts are still not paying
dividends, you now know some of the reasons why. Companies
whose efforts fail do so because they most often begin with the
hot technology, such as performance management systems,
electronic performance support systems, or video analysis.
They get all caught up in the latest and greatest technology

approaches to performance improvement and they forget the most important element. The one guaranteed way to make performance improvement work in any company of any size in any industry is to begin with the people. It's not the technology that makes it work, it's the people who use the technology. It's not mandating a corporate culture change to a measurement-centric organization that will make performance improvement work, it's the people who will enact and promote that culture change. So to be successful at performance improvement and to have any hope of guaranteeing it, **we must pay attention to the people.**

Good technology and bad people will not make for a successful performance improvement effort. Neither will good people and bad technology or a bad system. It takes great people, a solid plan, and then great performance technology within a great system. Then you'll get your results because you considered the people side of performance improvement first.

Guaranteeing Performance Improvement

In my work with corporations and individuals (athletes, business executives, salespeople, students, the general population), I have found a series of protocols or processes that guarantee performance improvement. The reason they work every time is that they focus on the person first. These approaches consider the whole performer first before applying the science of performance improvement. And the intriguing thing about them is that they are all extremely simple to apply. Yet we get so wrapped up in the science of what we do, we forget about the basics that always work.

The first thing that must be done to guarantee performance improvement is to help the performer answer the question "What's in it for me (WIIFM)?" Unless the performer sees, perceives, and believes there is a tangible emotional benefit to improving performance, he or she will not put forth the necessary effort. You must help the performer understand the **relevance** of the requirement for the improvement and the improvement itself.

Once relevance is established, you have to determine the performer's **set of beliefs**. We all come with two sets of beliefs: those that are enabling and those that are disabling. You must identify both sets of beliefs so that you can help the performer overcome the disabling beliefs. Unless these thoughts are out of the performer's mind, improvement is highly unlikely. In fact, you probably will witness significant performance decrements. Therefore, you must work with the performer to establish a strong set of enabling beliefs so that improvement can occur.

When the proper belief set has been established, help the performer identify the link between his or her own **value system** and the value of the improvement to the organization (and eventually, to society). Aligning the performer's personal values with the organization's values motivates the performer to give 100 percent effort to the task. If the performer does not see the value in improving, both to himself or herself and to the organization, then you will be engaging in an exercise in futility.

Finally, go back and apply the ideas mentioned in this chapter. Pay attention to the thoughts, emotions, mindsets, motivations, and perceptions of the performer. Never negate these or relegate them to second place behind some type of performance technology. Focus on the person first, and you'll be able to guarantee performance improvement in virtually any and every situation.

Endnotes

1.   The Gallup Organization has published several books on this concept. They heavily promote the strengths psychology approach. Don Clifton, the former chairman of Gallup is considered the father of strengths psychology. Some of the books they have published in this area include Buckingham, M., & Clifton, D., (2001). *Now, discover your strengths.* New York: Free Press; Buckingham, M., & Coffman, C., (1999). *First, break all the rules.* New York: Simon and Schuster; M. Buckingham, (2005). *The one thing you need to know.* New York: Free Press.

2.   Again, we see the power of positive reinforcement for proper task completion and successive approximations of task completion. The concept here is that the effort to succeed is reinforced as long as the result approaches the desired objective. This motivates performers to continue on with the task or repeat the task. Aubrey Daniels provides good coverage of these concepts in *Bringing Out The Best in People* (New York: McGraw-Hill, 1999) and *Other People's Habits* (New York: McGraw-Hill, 2000).

3.   While I have made this point several times in various articles in the *Performance Improvement Journal* for ISPI, see also my previous book, *Achieving High Performance: A Research-based Practical Approach* (Amherst, MA: HRD Press, 2006).

4.   The concept of focusing what you do, use, and produce on how it benefits society as a whole seems to be intuitively obvious. Yet, many people cannot get beyond their own microcosmic view of the world. That is unfortunate. Each person is a system unto herself, and this smaller system is part of an ever increasing larger system (group, team, or organization). All these systems make up the enterprise system we call society. So what one person does always has an effect, whether we realize it or see it or not, on society. This is the position Roger Kaufman has taken for over 40 years. For a review of these concepts, see one of his latest books, *Change, Choice and Consequences* (Amherst, MA: HRD Press, 2006).

5.   Jim Loehr has written extensively on the relationship between stress and performance. One of his earlier books still has valid applications today. *Stress for Success* (New York: Crown Books, 1997) discussed this relationship in both business and athletic settings.

Chapter 3
EI, PI, and ROI

They say that self-revelation for an author is cathartic. In this case, it is a personal story that helped shape part of my career. More than being cathartic, it has turned out to be highly motivating for the past 30 years. Take a trip with me down memory lane as we re-live how emotions affected a performance and how reframing the results had a beneficial effect.

A Speaker is Born

When I was a graduate student, I wrote a paper on athletic competition. In it, I stated that a definition of competition proposed by a world-famous sport psychologist, in a variety of publications, was inaccurate. Not incorrect, but inaccurate. I was encouraged to send the paper in for review for publication in a journal, and at the same time, to submit it as a presentation at a national conference. I was very reluctant at first, because I thought they would never accept a paper from a graduate student who was essentially saying a leader in the field didn't know what he was talking about. So, after much cajoling, I submitted the paper, never expecting to hear that it would be accepted.

Much to my surprise and chagrin, the paper was accepted. I was invited to present at the national conference as one of eight presenters, each of whom would have 15 minutes to present and answer questions. It was then I learned that the world-famous sport psychologist whom I said was inaccurate would be chairing the session and introducing the speakers. The conference was months away and I already was getting nervous. What would I say? How would I explain myself to him? What if he challenged me in front of the entire audience? You can readily see how I was building myself up to bomb at the presentation.

A few weeks before the conference, this world-famous sport psychologist called me (this was way before e-mail) to tell me that he was chairing the session and that he was very interested to hear what I had to say. In fact, he told me he couldn't wait. He was polite, professional, and very friendly. That didn't help me much, because now I was even more nervous. And conference time was approaching much faster than I had hoped for.

At the conference, the speakers who preceded me were all college professors who were used to speaking in front of an audience. This particular audience was 200 people (and it was my first professional presentation). I was fifth to present. I heard the person presenting before me apologize to the audience for not having his slides. They seemed to have gotten lost on the plane. I thought, "Oh great, now I'm supposed to have slides or overheads. What in the world am I doing here in front of all these professors?" You can imagine the mental and emotional state I was in.

Now it was my turn. The world-famous sport psychologist introduced me, and as I was walking up to the stage and he was walking off the other side, he stopped and said, "I can't wait to hear what Richard has to say." Just what I had to hear. As if I wasn't close to the edge already. But there was no turning back, so I began. I got behind the lectern, grabbed the sides with both hands in a death-like grip, took a deep breath, and said something stupid like my slides were also lost on the plane (or the dog ate them, or something like that). Obviously, I wasn't thinking clearly, and I had to give that 15-minute presentation. Why did I let them talk me into this?

So I began. And I proceeded to give them the best 15-minute presentation ever seen or heard at that national conference. Whether it was a professor, professional speaker, or student, I gave the best 15-minute presentation ever heard. I flew through that presentation so easily it was like I had wings. And when I was finished with my 15-minute presentation, **I still had 12 minutes left**. So I started to walk off the stage, and the world-famous sport psychologist said he had a question. Snap back to reality. Now what do I do? I thought I'd finished in record time and now he wants to ask me a question.

The truth be told, his question was not that bad and he complimented me on my presentation, although it was quite short. I said thank you and left the stage and the room, gasping for air. My nerves were shot, and I was hoping no one would come out and talk to me until I could catch my breath and compose myself.

And from this near-disaster, a speaker was born. Today, I speak in front of hundreds and thousands of people at a time without any fear, anxiety, or nervousness. Short or long, speech or workshop, I'm extremely comfortable when I'm in front of a group. I've come a long way from that first presentation. And it was all because I was able to master my nerves, emotions, and fears.

Emotions and Performance

There is a great deal of literature on emotions and performance. Rather than try to review and synthesize it here, let's focus on some things that we all know commonly affect performance and performance results. And let's relate them back to my speaking story. We must also pay close attention to the emotional states of performers. There are several issues at work here. The first is the effect of emotions on performance. We know from sports psychology[1] that a certain emotional arousal level is optimal for each performance, and this level differs depending on the difficulty of the task, the environment, and the skill level of the performer. We also know from memory research and motor skills research that learned skills are best recalled and performed when the performer is in a similar emotional state as when the task or material was originally learned. And finally, the entire emotional complexity that surrounds self-esteem determines how well someone will perform a task or on the job.[2]

The first thing we know about emotions and performance, or what has been called arousal in the motivational and psychological literature, is that too little or too much arousal hurts performance. If you are underaroused, you tend to be bored and lose concentration when you perform a task. If you are overaroused, you tend to "try too hard" and your thought processes and behaviors become "stunted." You are unable to perform with maximum efficiency and effectiveness. People who are constantly underaroused appear to be lethargic, sad, sullen, depressed, bored, lazy, and vegetating. People who are constantly overaroused appear to be nervous, anxious, fearful, angry, stressed out, hyper, and tense. While some of these emotional descriptors are often used in similar fashion, they are presented here separately so that you will realize the range of emotions a performer can go through in order to complete a task.

Now somewhere in between being underaroused and overaroused, you get into that optimal arousal (emotional) zone. This is the place where your emotions are under control, where you have the proper amount of "nervous tension" and "relaxed alertness." This is where you will experience a high-level performance, and even a peak performance. You might even enter into the flow state, where everything occurs almost effortlessly and without conscious intervention. You can do the task without thinking about it. You have achieved that optimal arousal zone and an ideal performance state. You feel great about what you are doing and will do, and what you have accomplished.[3]

How does this apply to my speaking story that opened the chapter? First, it is obvious that I was overaroused. In fact, I was wired. I was nervous, tense, anxious, scared to death, and who knows what else, all at the same time. Can you imagine the stress hormones that were running through my body at the time? It's a wonder I didn't explode. My overarousal led to a less than peak performance, that's for sure. It also led me to make the situation much worse than it actually was. I created all sorts of problems in my mind that negatively affected my performance. If I knew then what I know now about controlling emotions and "getting the butterflies to fly in formation," I might have been better off. I say "might" because I don't know if I would have become the speaker I am today without that poor performance.

There was a time during the speech where everything was flowing perfectly. Sometime during those three minutes that I was speaking, I blocked out the audience, the world-famous sport psychologist, and my lack of slides to get control of my nerves and at least say what I had to say in an intelligent fashion. So you might say that I achieved the optimal arousal zone for a short period of time. And this happens a lot, especially in sports. Take a championship basketball game for instance, or any sport or game for that matter. The players start out anxious and over-aroused. They make more mistakes than normal and the play is sloppy. Their adrenalin is pumping and they are making bad decisions. Then, after a period of time, they settle down into the flow of the game, get control of their emotions, and start to perform at a high level.

What this tells us is that emotions (and their related arousal states) work on a continuum and are constantly changing. They can be too high one minute and just right the next. The same is true for starting out too low on the arousal scale. Also, you can start out just right and then "lose it" somewhere along the way. In all cases, the emotional state of the performer has a tremendous affect on the performance, the result, and the accomplishment of performance objectives. That is why any attempt to guarantee performance improvement must consider the mental, emotional, psychological, and motivational state of the performer, regardless of the event, system, or setting in which the performance takes place.

The Emotional Side of Performance Improvement

The second issue we must consider is the emotional intelligence[4] of our performers, which we will talk about later in the chapter. Top performers must possess the ability to control their emotions properly given each specific performance situation, as well as to relate to others by understanding the emotional states of their co-workers. How well people control their own emotions and perform in the hailstorm of other people's emotions often distinguishes top performers from average performers. Furthermore, we, as performance improvement engineers or technologists, must match our emotional intelligence to the performer group we're trying to improve.

The third issue we must consider related to emotions and performance is how well people are dealing with their emotional demands and the stress of their performances. Excessive emotional demands can lead to a decrease in performance and a subsequent inability to learn or improve, while less emotionally demanding tasks or situations can actually lead to an improvement in performance. This is not to say that jobs should have no stress, because boredom and low arousal will lead to a decrease in task performance similar to the decrease caused by too much stress. And no matter what type of performance intervention you apply, you will not see the desired results if the performer's motivation, arousal, or stress levels are too low or too high. We will discuss the effects of stress on performance in Chapter 5.

I will describe both positive and negative emotions that you will encounter in performers when you're working with them to create improvements. I will conclude with a discussion of the benefits of dealing with the emotional side of performance improvement as perceived by the performer, as well as how to increase their desire and motivation to improve.

Emotional States

A performer's emotional state, regardless of whether it is positive or negative at the time of a performance, will affect four factors that are essential to effective performance. There are certainly other factors that are involved that influence the result of a performance. Things like resources, tools, environment, incentives, and others like that also affect performance. And as performance consultants, we are very tuned in to these factors. For our purposes, we will limit our discussion at this time to these four factors: attention, focus, perception, and time on task.

Attention refers to how well we tune in to the stimuli in our environment that are essential to successfully performing a task. We can attend to a broad or narrow range of stimuli, and we can consider all of them in a general context or a few of them in a specific context. This gives us an attentional style of either broad or narrow, and specific or general. Attention control is determined in part by the performer, the task, and the environment. For example, a basketball player shooting a foul shot must have a narrow and specific attention. A meeting facilitator must have a broad and general type of attention so that he or she pays attention to everything that is going on around the group. An electrician on a repair call must pay broad and general attention at first to find out what is wrong and to rule out other things, and then change to narrow and specific attention to complete the repairs.

It is intuitively obvious that how much attention a performer pays to a task influences and affects how well they perform. If their minds are elsewhere, because they are distracted or just not interested in their job, performance will suffer. If they are too present and their minds are too attentive (extremely narrow and specific), they will miss clues and cues that will help them perform well. Think of children in a classroom. There are so many things competing for their attention that it is difficult for many of them to concentrate on one particular task. So the teacher tells them to pay attention to the task, which they do for a while. Then they are distracted again, and the initial task performance suffers. The same holds true in the workplace.

What we must do to improve performance in this situation is help people concentrate their attention on the task at hand, minimize distractions if distractions will be harmful, and then teach them to take their attention to the next level.[5]

The next level requires that they be able to focus on what they are doing. Focus requires an almost laser-like state of concentration. While this has been called mindfulness in some circles,[6] we should call it **mind fullness**. Our minds must be **full** with the task at hand, or in other words, fully focused on the task at hand. You can call it concentration or paying attention or being totally present, but it is actually a little more. When you ask performers to focus, you are asking them to stay tuned in to what they must do regardless of what is occurring around them. They must block out distractions and other competing stimuli. Basketball players must block out the waving towels and signs as they shoot a foul shot so that they make the shot rather than miss. Football and basketball teams practice in stadiums and arenas with crowd noise being piped in for this exact reason. The coaches want their players to remain focused on the task at hand despite the ongoing distractions of other things competing for each performer's attention. We can help people dramatically improve their performances if we just help them maintain the proper focus through emotional control.

The level of emotional control will affect a performer's perception of the situation. People who are very upset or angry tend to perceive things differently than those who are relaxed. And people who are in a state of optimal arousal (emotional control) perceive events differently from everyone else. In fact, when you are in a state of optimal emotional arousal, you can experience that state of flow that was mentioned before. A person is in flow when his or her attention is properly focused, the task is challenging, and his or her emotions are in an optimal arousal state. Plus, the performer is just letting the performance happen with minimal or no conscious intervention. In other words, they are not thinking about what they are doing, they are just doing it. And they are doing it at the highest level possible.[7]

When performers are in flow, their perceptions become very acute. Time and motion seem to slow down, movement and thought become effortless, and positive emotions flood the mind-body system. If we can help people achieve this state of flow more often, their overall performances and productivity will greatly improve. One of the ways we can do this is to create a task that is challenging and meaningful and, when properly completed, will positively affect the performer's self-esteem.

The last area that the emotional state of the performer affects is the time on task. When someone is in a flow state, they can perform indefinitely. Since "time stands still," they just keep on going. However, when the performer is in a negative emotional state, they will do anything to get away from the task. Minutes drag on like hours, and every activity related to completing the task is drudgery. The negative emotional state begins to cycle on itself and cause a continuing decrease in performance.

This requires a change in the job, the reward, or the recognition system for performing the job, the environment, or the praising system (which is another way of saying you should tell people when they're doing a good job). It's not that we are trying to increase the time on task so that a person stays on the job indefinitely. The real goal is to determine the time required to effectively complete the task and make sure that the performer is in the proper emotional state to remain at the job and perform it well for the time required.

Negative Emotions That Hinder Performance

While there are many negative emotions that can affect performance, we should consider these ten as the primary obstacles to performance improvement:

1. **Fear.** This is a perceptual event that occurs because the performer does not have control over the situation and also might not know the result of certain behaviors. Simply put, there are too many unknowns. In most cases, fear is nothing more than **F**alse **E**xpectations **A**ppearing **R**eal.

2. **Anxiety.** The tension produced by a situation where there is uncertainty, unpredictability, a perceived lack of control, too much pressure, a lack of skills, or a threat to a person's self-esteem results in anxiety.

3. **Anger** (which leads to aggression). This is a natural emotion that is most often manifested in negative ways, either through physical or verbal abuse, yelling or screaming, turning red in the face, or punching a hole in a wall. Sometimes, anger is also displayed as passive-aggressive behavior.

4. **Frustration.** This feeling is simply because the performer cannot control the result of the performance,

either because the situational environment is limiting or the skill set is lacking. Basically, the performer is doing everything she can to succeed, but she is just not quite getting there.

5. **Sadness.** An inability to perform well or achieve a goal can lead to feelings of sadness or despair. Other factors can also cause sadness, such as repeatedly missing the mark, losing, self-doubt, and actual low feelings that precede depression.

6. **Depression.** When sadness gets too great, depression results. In a performance situation, it is usually the result of continued failure, knocks to self-esteem, a sense of loss, a feeling you cannot overcome certain obstacles, or just giving up.

7. **Detachment.** People tend to alienate themselves from others for a variety of reasons. When performers feel they don't belong or are not part of the team or go unrecognized for their efforts and accomplishments, they detach from the performance situation as well as the people around them.

8. **Confusion** (a mental state more so than an emotion). Too much stress, anxiety, fear, or any of the negative emotions results in an inability to make decisions, make choices, or effectively complete a task. Sometimes things get so bad that a person thinks his or her brain will explode because of all the competing tendencies (too many things requiring the attention of the performer) that are causing the confusion.

9. **Shame.** This occurs when a performer is embarrassed by not completing a task or doing well at an assignment. It usually relates to how the performer feels others will perceive him or her. Very often, shame is an internal emotion because no one else is shaming the performer or trying to make the performer feel bad. It is a self-interpretation.

10. **Distraction** (another mental state). This results from an inability to maintain concentration and focus on the task at hand. The performer might have other things on his mind, including personal issues not related to the task in front of him. People also get distracted when there are too many instructions being thrown at them on how to perform a task.

Each of these negative emotions or mental states is harmful to performance or attempts at improvement. They slow learning, they adversely affect performance, and they ultimately perpetuate a negative cycle. Once a negative emotion is repeatedly linked (anchored) to a poor performance or an inability to improve, it tends to strengthen that negative relationship. This then leads to other negative emotions and feelings of helplessness or unworthiness creeping over the performer. Next, self-esteem is lowered and performance continues to decrease. Ultimately, the performer just cannot seem to learn how to improve the performance. This is the proverbial "death spiral" or vicious cycle.

At this point, all the technical and technological interventions in the world will not help. It's as if the person has given up on improving performance. It then becomes our job to first create an environment where the performer feels safe and experiences a series of successful events, and where positive emotions flourish. Once that is done, then and only then should we consider working on improving performances.

Positive Emotions That Help Performance

Again, we can look at a host of positive emotions that will help improve performance. Unfortunately, people seem to be able to name more negative emotions than positive ones. They have to look a little harder and a little deeper to find the positive emotions that come in to play when someone is performing well. If you or people you are working with are having difficulty identifying positive emotions related to performance, then go out and just ask people who are experiencing flow (or are in the "zone") what else they are feeling.

Here are ten positive emotions or motivational states that we should all strive to activate when we are engaged in an actual performance or we are trying to create a performance improvement situation. They are:

1. **Joy/Happiness/Elation.** This is one of the most natural emotions and one that is not experienced often enough during any type of performance. When performing is fun, happiness naturally follows because of the intrinsic satisfaction derived from the performance. You can also artificially create this feeling by having the performer succeed at some task and then smile as you review the successful results. This anchors the smile to the outcome and becomes the trigger for performance-related happiness.

2. **Achievement motivation** (and risk-taking behavior). This is a measurable construct that tells us how much risk a person is willing to take in order to achieve a goal. Most performers are comfortable with moderate risk that slightly challenges them. Too much or too little risk presents a problem, just as too much or too little arousal also hinders performance.

3. **Approach motivation** (actively seeking results). People either approach or avoid situations. This is the positive side of the motivation continuum. While most people prefer to seek pleasure, in actuality, they will do more to avoid pain than seek or achieve gain. It's part of human nature to move away from what is hurting you.

4. **Appreciation.** This is the number one desire of all people. We show appreciation in many ways, and the more ways and times we show it to performers, the better they will perform. In fact, appreciation and recognition have been known to elevate perform-ances very rapidly, turn organizational cultures around, and build more positive relationships among workers and supervisors.

5. **Relaxation** (both mental and physical). This has been shown to be highly effective at reducing stress, increasing visualization abilities, and improving performance in a variety of endeavors. Since relaxation and tension (anxiety, fear, pressure) cannot co-exist simultaneously, you will always be in a more prepared state to perform if you are relaxed. That is, of course, unless you get too relaxed.

6. **Confidence.** This is the feeling people have when they truly believe in themselves and their ability to achieve goals. Self-confidence can elevate performance to levels much higher than any training program or other performance intervention. It is also the one major factor that contributes to either winning streaks (having confidence) or losing streaks (not having confidence).

7. **Engagement** (absorption in a performance). This is when performers are totally involved with what they are doing. It is part of the flow concept, the optimal arousal level for performance, and having a commitment to your task.

8. **Faith** (and a positive belief system). You "gotta" believe in something, so it might as well be yourself and your capabilities. Faith also provides you with enabling beliefs, those statements you make to yourself that "help get you through the night" (or at least the performance). Then believe in the improvement interventions, and success is inevitable.

9. **Pride.** This is the feeling that accompanies accomplishment. Being proud of yourself for doing well helps you grow as a performer and increases your desire to perform again as well as your motivation to do well.

10. **Enthusiasm.** This positive feeling you have toward a task and its accomplishment also leads to peak performances, happiness, and a great deal of self-

esteem. Being motivated to do something and to do it well very often results in better than expected results.

Focus on these positive emotions in the performers you are trying to influence and you will generate significant improvements. There is one thing you must realize about emotions and motivation, though. No one can really create emotions in someone else nor can they motivate someone else. The only thing we can do as performance improvement specialists is to create the conditions that will enable someone to motivate themselves, to feel good about themselves, and to expect to succeed. This expectancy of success will lead to greater and greater confidence in future performances along with an increased desire to constantly improve. As long as we provide the right conditions, performance improvement will occur. Sometimes this improvement will be incremental, and other times it will be a quantum leap. In any case, it will occur as long as the performer is in a positive emotional state.

In summary, you want to increase some emotions and decrease others (see table below). As you can see from inspecting this table, these emotions are basically polar opposites. The positive ones will most often improve performance while the negative ones will usually hinder performance. When you increase the positive emotional aspects related to a performance, you increase the psychological and physical energy levels of performers, their expectancy of success, their levels of self-esteem, their motivation to do whatever it takes to get better (i.e., commitment), and their ability to learn and perform new tasks.

Emotions to Improve Performance

Increase These Emotions to Improve Performance	Decrease These Emotions to Improve Performance
Joy	Sadness
Happiness	Depression
Hope	Hopelessness
Love	Hate
Faith	Despair
Pride	Selfishness
Confidence	Egotism
Security	Insecurity
Courage	Fear
Self-Satisfaction	Jealousy/Envy

One other point I want to make here involves the concept of security. I am not talking about job security. I am talking about emotional security. This involves allowing the performer to know that he or she can make mistakes and learn from them. It requires that performers not be punished for "failing" to exhibit a peak performance every time. And it enables performers to "fail forward." We all make mistakes in life. Most of them are not earth shattering or mind blowing, yet bosses, colleagues, or parents berate us for them. I am suggesting we consider the situation the mistake was made in, consider the emotional state of the performer, and consider the outcome that occurred. Then we make a determination about how we are going to handle the person and the situation.

Our reaction to any individual's performance often determines whether or not that person will perform again. Think of a toddler learning to walk. As parents, we applaud each step, voice encouragement, and even provide "job aids" (things they can hold on to, role models, and mechanical devices such as walkers) to help them perform better. Despite hundreds of failures, children still continue to pick themselves up one more time than they fall down, and eventually, they improve enough to walk.

We must treat performers the same way. If you coach little league sports, you know exactly what I'm talking about when I say use positive reinforcement to generate improvements. You should use the same type of motivation and encouragement in the workplace with adults that you use with children. If you teach Sunday school or religious classes, use the same type of encouragement. Take care of your workers' emotions the same way you take care of your children's or players' emotions. Your goal in every situation is to help the performer achieve continual improvement and continued success.

EI and PI: Emotional Intelligence and Performance Improvement

There is probably no other topic in the past 10 to 15 years that has received the type of voluminous coverage as the concept of emotional intelligence (EI). While research into this area began in the 1980s, it wasn't until Daniel Goleman popularized the term and tied the existing literature together in 1995 that emotional intelligence started to gain traction outside academic communities. In fact, EI has become so popular that people are saying it can replace IQ as a predictor of performance success in many areas. EI is also being used now in making hiring decisions at all levels of a corporation, as well as determining who will fit in well with a team or a group. There are even some compatibility tests on the Internet that address emotional intelligence.[8] Wherever you go, you can't escape the universality of EI at this time.

While the concept has evolved over the years, it is generally accepted that there are four major categories of emotional intelligence within which exist 20 mini-domains or competencies. The four primary categories are self-awareness, self-management, social awareness, and relationship management. Self-awareness is defined as a deep understanding of your own emotions, strengths, and weaknesses, and an ability to accurately and honestly assess yourself. Self-awareness is like giving yourself a private 360-degree assessment so that you know yourself better than anybody. Self-management refers to the control and regulation of your emotions; the ability to stay calm, clear, and focused even under pressure or when a performance does not go as you planned it; and the ability for self-motivation and to take personal initiative. The second two domains are social and concern a performer's ability to manage relationships with others. Social awareness includes empathy, the ability to consider the feelings of others while making intelligent decisions either on a one-to-one basis or as a group, and knowing how what you do, use, and produce affects others, including individuals, groups, organizations, and society. Relationship management is your ability to communicate effectively, influence positively, collaborate and work with colleagues, plus keep relationships on an even and positive keel over time.

Close on the heels of EI and how it affects performance is the concept of practical intelligence (PI). Practical intelligence is a person's ability to select which environments to perform in, adapt to that environment, and even shape or modify that environment. PI includes a person's tacit knowledge (what she holds in her mind) as well as a demonstrable ability to perform successfully in a variety of areas, including work, sports, personal life, and school. While there has not been as much work on PI as there has been on EI, PI does make intuitive sense as we can see actual performance differences between experts and novices and how they describe their thought processes. In all cases, the combination presents a powerful tool for performance improvement professionals.

How to Use Emotional and Practical
Intelligence for Performance Improvement

If we are helping someone improve their performance, we must engage them in a conversation about their emotional state at the time. We have to know how aware they are of what they are feeling and thinking, plus how confident they are that they can control both their positive and negative emotions that may occur during a performance. We also must help them understand the individual, group, organizational, and societal benefits of their performance, especially if it requires that they work with someone else. Additionally, every performer has some knowledge of what to do and how to do it. We have to help them advance that knowledge so that they can one day become expert performers and perform in their optimal arousal zone. It would be even better if we could help them turn that tacit (implicit) knowledge into explicit knowledge so that they could explain it to others and coach others on how to be top performers.

Let's return again to my first professional presentation. If I had someone to help me with my emotional and practical intelligence, the performance coaching session may have gone something like this: My coach would have asked me how I felt about the presentation, probably discussing where my attention was focused and how confident I was. I can tell you that I had a narrow and specific focus of attention, and it was all directed inward. That's what was causing my stress and anxiety. Add to that the fact that I was well aware that I lacked the confidence to do a good job, and you have the recipe for disaster. Plus, I didn't have any way to control my emotions because I was so locked in to "surviving" not "thriving" during the presentation. And I was very concerned about how people would perceive me "when I blew the presentation," which I was sure I would do.

So my coach would have helped me find something I was confident in doing, ask me about a situation where I was able to effectively manage my emotions and perform well (like the time I scored 56 points in a playoff game in a basketball league), and discuss a time when I spoke with people and had a positive effect on them. This would have helped me activate my emotional intelligence. Then my coach would have talked with me about what I knew about speaking to groups on a topic that I was familiar with. We would have also talked about how I could make the presentation room "more friendly" as well as talk to a few friends in the audience when I was up on stage. Using this approach, my coach would have helped me increase both my emotional intelligence and practical intelligence to achieve a high-level performance.

By the way, this is one of the personal approaches I use for myself and my coaching clients when I help them make a presentation to an audience. There are many other emotion management techniques, some of which we'll talk about in the next chapter on stress and performance. The important point is to realize that emotions play a vital role in the success or failure of a performance. We have to manage them for ourselves and for the people we are working with. This is especially important with executives, salespeople, athletes, students, and managers. In fact, better emotion management will lead to better and more effective performances.

Gaining Emotional Mastery

The goal for every performer is to gain and maintain mastery over their emotions, both positive and negative. Without judging which type of emotion may be at work during a performance, it is enough to say that too much or too little of any emotion is probably going to be detrimental to performance. So the key factor is to gain mastery over your emotions. You do this by increasing your self-awareness plus practicing emotional control. With every type of physical performance—be it work, sports, dance, or anything else—perfect practice will lead to perfect performance. And all great performers practice on a regular basis. The same must be said for emotional mastery. To get good at it, you must practice it on a regular basis. If you are a manager or team leader, you must create an environment for your team members to be able to perfectly practice their skills so that they too can achieve emotional mastery.

Start by becoming aware of how you respond to a given situation. Which emotions occur and become noticeable prior to, during, and after a performance? Increasing your self-awareness will go a long way to helping you develop the skills to master and control your emotions. This will also improve your perspective and perception of each performance situation. When you perceive a situation more realistically, there is less of a chance of activating emotions that could hurt or hinder your performance. A realistic appraisal of yourself and your situation will help you achieve higher levels of performance because you will be able to identify and control the emotions that occur.

There are several approaches you can use to gain your emotional mastery. The first one is choice. You actually can choose to feel good or bad during or after a performance. You can choose to be anxious or relaxed. And you can choose to be positive or negative. The difficulty with using choice to control your emotions is sometimes you have no choice. You have been ingrained to respond in certain ways in certain situations and the emotional response "fires off" automatically. It is when this happens that you must develop some other type of intervention for emotional control.

Assuming you are able to assess and identify the emotions that are affecting your performance, I suggest you take what is called a "third-party observer" position. This lets you look at your situation more objectively and allows you to evaluate it as if you were someone else. Placing yourself in the position of an outside evaluator will help you see the forest for the trees. This objective outlook will also help you choose a different or better performance path because your choices are not being ruled by negative or over-aroused emotions.

If you find it difficult to be this objective and detached and you can't seem to "get away" from the emotional effects, you can use a technique called dissociation. Basically, dissociation allows you to "dis-associate" yourself from the situation. When you do this, the situation (performance) has no apparent emotional meaning for you and you are able to perform it without being hindered by negative emotions. People who have to dis-associate themselves tend to talk in "I" terms, saying things like "I screwed up," or "I'm no good at this," or "It's all my fault."

They take responsibility and self-blame when they do not have to or should not have to do it. This leads to negative emotional cycles, such as frustration, anger, defeat, and hopelessness. You have to reappraise the situation and look for the positives in every performance no matter what the outcome if you want to consistently achieve high performance and guarantee performance improvement. Therefore, step back, use dissociation, and reappraise your situation.

Another approach I use a great deal with my coaching clients is the power of positive self-talk. I help them identify and define statements (either self-directed dialog or affirmations) that will make them feel better about themselves. While these affirmations may seem simplistic, and you may doubt their effect on a performer and future performances, I urge you to try them for yourself. Saying positive things to yourself will, after a time, cause your mind to start believing those things. Your self-esteem will increase, your self-confidence will increase, and your self-image will become more positive. All these things will then have a positive and beneficial effect on future performances. You will be pleasantly surprised at the good feelings you will experience after using affirmations for a few days.

The simple protocol to make this work for you is to write out five positive affirmations or self-talk statements. Then repeat these to yourself at least twice a day, every day. In a few days, you will start to believe these things about yourself and you will see an improvement in your performance. Your increased self-confidence will be evident in your higher performance levels.

Mastering your emotions to help you improve performance and achieve ever-increasing levels of performance is critical to your success. Use the chart below to test yourself to see how often you use these techniques for emotional mastery. A good friend of mine, Dr. Jack Wolf, talks about how we behave and perform "up till now" and "from now on." I have used his terms instead of *present/current* and *future/will do* in the chart. So check off what you have been doing up until now and what you will do from now on.

Emotional Mastery	Up Till Now	From Now On
Self-awareness		
Third-party observer		
Dissociation		
Positive self-talk		
Positive affirmations		

Everything that has been mentioned above for you, the reader, is exactly what you should do for your team members if you manage or coach them. You just transfer the skills that you've developed for yourself to them through coaching, role modeling, or mentoring. Remember, it is rare that one top performer can carry a team to high levels of performance on a regular basis. It is even more rare for that one top performer to be able to guarantee performance improvement for her team if the team members are not trained in the skills of emotional mastery. You must work on this together, first for yourself and then with the people you work or play with.

The Last Word

The last word on dealing with the emotional side of performance improvement is simple: You cannot ignore the *effect that affect* has on performance. Stimulate your performers, support their efforts, help them motivate themselves, and you will see performance improvements and performance results that were previously thought impossible. What they will achieve when they are provided emotional security, support for their self-esteem, and a challenging task to perform (which includes clear performance objectives) will go beyond the results that the typical technical and technological tools, models, and theories provide. They will definitely achieve beyond your expectations and, sometimes, even their own expectations. That's because their emotions are involved and effectively managed, they are committed to getting better as performers, and they know they will continue to feel good about themselves after repeated successes.

Using emotional intelligence and emotional mastery will lead to performance improvements. Performance improvements that occur on a regular basis because the performer has control over his or her emotions will lead to a positive return on investment, in monetary terms as well as performer confidence, loyalty, and productivity. The three concepts of EI, PI, and ROI are intertwined when you are focusing on guaranteeing performance improvement.

Endnotes

1.   Gerson, R. F., (2004). *HEADcoaching: Mental training for peak performance*. Bloomington, IN: Authorhouse.

2.   Branden, N., (1998). *Self-esteem at work*. San Francisco, CA: Jossey-Bass.

3.   There is a voluminous amount of literature on this topic. Here are just a few resources for you to consider. You can also place any of the terms mentioned in this paragraph into a search engine to identify more resources. You can read Csikszentmihalyi, M., (1977). *Finding flow*. New York: Basic Books; Gerson, R. F., (1998). *Winning the inner game of selling*. Menlo Park, CA: Crisp Publications; Loehr, J., (1997). *Stress for success*. New York: Random House; Gerson, R. F., (2004). *HEADcoaching: Mental training for peak performance*. Bloomington, IN: Authorhouse; Gerson, R. F., (2006). *Achieving high performance: A research-based practical approach*. Amherst, MA: HRD Press.

4. Daniel Goleman has written extensively on this topic. Although he was not the first to research the topic, he was the first to get emotional intelligence accepted into the popular culture or mainstream business language. You can find multiple references, such as books, articles, and white papers at www.eiconsortium. org.

5. The different types of attention and how to change focus were "made famous" in the sports world with applications to business by Robert Nideffer. He talked about controlling attention, narrowing and expanding it, in his book *Psyched to Win* (Champaign, IL: Human Kinetics, 1992).

6. See, for example, the work of Ellen Langer of Harvard University, who has done a great deal of research on mindfulness and performance. Her initial book, *Mindfulness* (Boston: Addison Wesley, 1990) and her second book, *The Power of Mindful Learning* (Boston: Addison Wesley, 1997) cover this topic in detail.

7. Refer back to the Csikszentmihalyi reference in Note 3, as well as Jackson, S., & Csikszentmihalyi, M., (1999). *Flow in sports.* Champaign, IL: Human Kinetics.

8. For those of you who are interested in these relationship building sites, you can check out www.eharmony.com, www.match.com, and www.perfectmatch.com. Mentioning these sites is not an endorsement of them or anything they claim to do.

Chapter 4
Seven Steps to Guaranteeing Performance Improvement: The GET RICH Approach

Now this is a scary thought: How could anyone *guarantee* performance improvement or positive results of any kind? Don't most consultants come into a company, employ a process that they expect to work because it may have worked somewhere else once before, and then leave it up to the company to actually make it work? Then when the company doesn't get the results they wanted, the consultants, who by now are usually long gone and on to their next assignment, tell the company that they probably didn't follow the process properly. While there are certain problems inherent in any process approach, it is always easy to lay out a process and blame the end user for not following it perfectly to get the desired results. Wouldn't it be nice, if just once, someone would guarantee that they could get you the results you desire and deserve?

Here's another example from the advertising industry: Advertising agencies make money on placing ads in addition to their creative work. Most agencies receive a commission on the costs of the ads. There are very few agencies that will work on the basis of a percentage of the incremental revenues their advertising brings in for their client. This variable rate concept, which is literally a pay-for-performance program, is not well liked or used by most ad agencies. They want to be paid for their process because they can't guarantee their results. In fact, most people would like to be paid for their process rather than the performance. This way, they have little to no accountability or responsibility for the result. When you "pay for performance," you are forcing the performer (or the provider) to guarantee positive results. The real question is how do we get people comfortable with the concept of guaranteeing performance improvement?

Improving Performance by
Increasing Respect

Many years ago, I was asked to help a hospital improve the performance of their emergency room staff. The situation was simple: Patient satisfaction ratings were on the decline and no previous interventions had stopped the slide. The hospital had tried organizational restructuring, rewriting job descriptions, and "morale" training. They had the top doctors and nurses in their county on staff who provided excellent care. Yet none of the interventions worked as the satisfaction ratings kept dropping. When I was asked to help them, they thought they had exhausted all their potential interventions and solutions. They wanted me to come up with a systematic (process-oriented) and systemic (comprehensive) solution. After all, I had written several books on customer service and satisfaction, so I should be able to help them raise their satisfaction ratings. And their asking for a systematic and systemic approach was right out of the "HPT handbook," even though they did not know it at the time.

The problem was they had tried to improve the satisfaction ratings using different process approaches. Teams were formed and re-formed. Schedules were reworked to accommodate staff. Department heads and senior officers were told to be nicer to the ER staff. The ER staff received "smile" training and were told to be nicer to the patients and their families. Yet none of these interventions gave them the desired results of increased patient satisfaction. So armed with all this knowledge about what was tried and had failed to produce positive and useful results, I made a suggestion to the executive vice president who called me in. My suggestion was that he could pay me an agreed-upon fee for my work, regardless of the results we achieved. Or he could pay me a lesser amount for the project, and when the desired results were achieved (which was an increase of at least 3 percent in the patient satisfaction ratings within the next quarter), he would pay me double the original amount. Since nothing was working, he agreed to my proposal. Maybe he thought I would fail just like the other interventions failed. What he didn't know is that I have a different approach in situations like this.

I went to the emergency room and spent portions of several days observing the staff: front desk staff, nurses, EMTs, doctors, orderlies, and anyone else who contributed to the effective functioning of the ER. There was no problem with the running of the ER—it functioned like a well-oiled machine. The problem that I discovered was between the doctors and the nurses. They simply did not respect each other. During individual interviews and small group sessions, each group bad-mouthed the other one. While they did their jobs together and took great care of the patients, they did not really like each other. That was because they did not truly respect each other.

The nurses thought the doctors were lazy, quick to blame the nurses for anything that went wrong, and great at taking all the credit for a successful patient treatment. The doctors thought the nurses didn't respect their authority. What I found out was that the two groups simply **did not respect each other as individuals**. So my task was to come up with an intervention that would work and work quickly. Here's what I did.

I had the doctors and nurses switch responsibilities wherever feasible. Doctors would now take basic blood pressures and health histories, answer phones, and change the linens in the ER. Nurses would interview the patients and talk with the families, plus prepare to make the patient's diagnosis. While the nurses loved the "job switching," the doctors hated it. They finally realized that the nurses had a tough and important job to do. They just never knew how tough it really was until they stepped into the shoes of the nurses.

Now that everyone had a newfound appreciation for the other group's work, they began to treat each other better as individuals. This niceness among the staff was picked up by the patients, who began to rate the ER higher on satisfaction surveys. The end result was that through this individualized intervention, performance improved, patient satisfaction ratings increased, and I was paid double my fee. All in all, it worked out well for everyone.

Pay Attention to the Person

This example—and hundreds of others from my career and the experiences of other consultants—tells you time and again to pay close attention to the person doing the performance. The organization and the system within which it functions are very important, and so is the individual performer. While a poor system may stymie a star performer, a reluctant performer will stymie a superior system. You must determine what makes the performer tick in all cases in order to make a performance intervention work. Plus, you must provide the appropriate conditions for that performer to feel comfortable completing the performance. In short, you must pay attention to the person doing the performance.[1]

Every person brings certain things to every performance. There is a set of attitudes, values, and beliefs that drive a person to engage in an activity. There is the feeling of self-confidence or self-doubt that affects a performance. There is a history of previous results from similar performance that shape the person's perceptions about how well she will do this time. And there is the current skill set the performer possesses.

Now it would be ridiculous to put a person in a situation where he did not have the skills to complete the job at a high level. For example, there is no way on earth I could win an American Idol contest, so all the interventions (music training, voice training, vocal practice) will never make me a winner. Except for the fact that I am not shy about getting up on stage in front of people (my speaking and training skills help here), I would have no chance to be successful. However, I could win a foul shooting contest since I have played basketball for way too many years. So the mindset I would bring to each situation would be vastly different. I would go to American Idol with a "positive" defeatist attitude, knowing there was no way I could win. I would go to the foul shooting contest fully believing that I would win, no matter who was in it. The difference in my skill sets and previous experiences influences my mindset about my performance. And no type of systematic or systemic intervention will change that or the result.

So what do we do? How do we get people to elevate their performances to such a level that we—as managers, business owners, or consultants—can actually guarantee performance improvement? The answer is really very simple, but it is not easy. We have to pay attention to the performer and follow these seven steps. The steps are not really a process. They are more like things you should do for, to, and with the performer to guarantee improvement. The seven steps also form the mnemonic *GET RICH*. The letters stand for:

Goal setting
Expectation management
Talent optimization
Recognition
Imagination
Concentration
Habituation

Here is how you GET RICH and virtually guarantee performance improvement.

Goal Setting and Establishing Performance Objectives

You are probably familiar with the concept of SMART goal setting. This means that your goals must be Specific, Measurable, Accomplishment-based, Realistic, and Time-based. You must specifically state what you want to accomplish, make sure the statement includes a measurement component, be certain you have the skills to achieve the realistic objective, and do so within a reasonable time frame. For example, a performance goal (or objective, as it can also be called) for a salesperson would be to increase sales by 10 percent during the next quarter as measured by gross revenues. A performance goal for a department could be to increase customer satisfaction ratings by 3 percent over the next quarter. And a performance goal for a company could be to increase customers in a specific market segment by 5 percent during the next six months. The key is that you specify the measurable results and consequences so that you can evaluate the end performance and make any changes that are necessary for future performances. SMART goal and objective setting is, simply, smart.

Since this is a practical applications book, let's try a simple goal setting exercise that you can use immediately. Consider the five SMART characteristics of goals and write down a performance goal for something you have to do very soon. You should actually do this for several upcoming tasks, because this will get you in the habit of goal setting for performance planning. You already do something like this when you plan a vacation. In fact, most people spend more time planning their vacations and setting goals that have to be achieved relative to that vacation than they do planning for their work or some other aspect of their lives. Write down your performance goal below and check it for the SMART characteristics:

_____

_____

_____

_____

_____

Recently, a more expansive approach to goal and objective setting has been proposed, called SMARTER goal setting.[2] This approach adds a few more dimensions to the goal and objective setting process while taking into account the concept of "stretch" objectives. It also forces us to make objectives more exact and rigorous, which turns them into true performance objectives. These performance objectives allow us to determine exactly what we want to achieve, how we will achieve it, and how we will measure our success. There are still similarities between SMARTER objectives and SMART goals and objectives. For example, they both must still be **S**pecific and **M**easurable.

In this new model, however, they should also be **A**udacious, which the authors describe as super-stretch goals. We see this concept of audacious goal setting in what has been called BHAG (Big, Hairy, Audacious Goals)[3] and "realistically impossible" goals.[4] The intent here is to definitely take people out of their comfort zones and get them to achieve things they never thought possible. This audacious concept makes a great deal of sense because you always want to motivate or help motivate a performer to do better than he or she thought possible. The first R in SMARTER objectives refers to **R**esults. Here the performance is described in terms of what will be achieved, rather than how something will be achieved. Proper performance objectives refer to end results rather than means, activities, processes, or behaviors. The objectives must also be **T**ime bound. You must be able to achieve them within a specified time period. Your time frame will also be affected by making the goals/objectives **E**xpansive, which means you will be concerned with both the system and systemic effects of your accomplishments. This also allows you to link the goals/objectives to the Mega/Macro/Micro objectives you set (see previous references to Kaufman). Finally, SMARTER objectives must be written so that you can **R**eview and evaluate the results. You want to review and evaluate constantly throughout a performance so that you can make changes, adjustments, and improvements; identify strengths and weaknesses; and determine any differential effects that might occur.

The challenge is to not only be SMART with your goal and objective setting, it is also to now be SMARTER than everyone else. You will see your performance levels measurably increase when you do this, plus your self-confidence will grow as you accomplish more. And the more your self-confidence grows, the higher your subsequent levels of performance.[5]

Here is an example to test your knowledge of the SMARTER objective setting process. Read the following brief scenario about a customer service representative and then answer the questions either yes or no to determine if the statement fits the criteria for being SMARTER.

Scenario: The company has set an objective that all call center reps will increase first-call resolution (FCR) completed calls by at least 7 percent. Joan, a top CSR, has written her objective statement down as "I will increase my FCR calls by at least 10 percent in the next 12 months."		
	YES	NO
Was Joan's goal/objective stated specifically?		
Will Joan be able to measure her performance related to the achievement of her objective?		
Is her statement audacious compared to what the company wants?		
Are the results of the performance stated clearly?		
Has the statement specified a time frame in which to achieve the objective?		
Will the achievement of the goal have an effect on the organization in addition to Joan?		
Does the statement provide either a point in time to review the performance or a methodology to review the performance?		

If you answered yes to all the questions, then you believe that the scenario statement is a SMARTER performance goal/objective, and you would be correct. While it takes some time to write out measurable performance goals and objectives in this manner, it is definitely more effective because you specify the behavior, the results, and the measurement to achieve the results. The only thing you do not specify is the method, means, activities, or actions to achieve the result. Although most goal setting training programs (and objective setting) tell you that you have to write down how you will achieve the desired result, you are actually limiting yourself when you do this. You are proposing or promoting a solution that might lock you in to a way of being or doing and lock you out of alternative approaches, some of which might be more effective than the one you selected. And this is also a problem when we determine an intervention for a performance improvement by focusing more on the system instead of or without focusing on the individual.

For example, in the objective statement in the chart, if we added the phrase "by spending only 2 to 3 minutes on each call" to the end of the statement, we would have specified the method of achievement, which would then cause the CSR to focus on speeding up the call completion without regard for results or consequences. We would be leaving out other possible approaches, such as self-service for call-in customers, preemptive calls to determine the status of the product, or agent routing, where certain calls are routed to agents with specific skill sets to resolve the calls quickly and to the caller's satisfaction. When you write out your true goal or objective statement, just state how you will know when you've arrived—the measurement that tells you the result has been achieved. Leave the methods and means for a later analysis and implementation.

Remember this about a performance goal/objective: The goal or objective specifies what result is to be accomplished, who or what will demonstrate the accomplishment, under what conditions the performance will be observed, and what criteria will be used to measure success. It does not specify how (the one way) you will get there.

Another Approach to Goal Setting

I recommend another approach called the A-O-I method (Acceptable, Outstanding, Ideal) of goal and objective setting. This approach takes into account people's perceptions of their abilities and their willingness to accept certain levels of performance. Each level of the A-O-I method must be stated as SMARTER goals also. The first level is **A**cceptable goals and objectives. These levels of results or achievements are minimally acceptable by the performer. It is the baseline measure that will minimally satisfy the performer that she accomplished something worthwhile. For example, a machine operator might set a minimally **A**cceptable objective of completing the workday with only eight or fewer minor mistakes per day. Of course, a lot depends on how this operator defines minor mistakes. But, for now, let's just leave it as an example. Going on from there, the machine operator might set an **O**utstanding objective of only four or fewer minor mistakes per day. This reduces his error rate by at least 50 percent and should increase productivity, which would help the organization. The final objectives should be to operate the machine in an **I**deal fashion and make no mistakes during the day. What are your **A**cceptable, **O**utstanding, and **I**deal goals and objectives for what you do?

Acceptable performance goal: _____

_____

_____

_____

Outstanding performance goal: _____

_____

_____

_____

Ideal performance goal: _____

_____

_____

_____

Expectation Management

Expectations are our beliefs about our probabilities for success. They are based on a variety of factors, including but not limited to previous successful experiences, knowledge of the task to be performed, attitudes, potential rewards and consequences for the results achieved upon completing the task based on previous similar experiences, external influences such as the performance environment, what other people tell us we should believe, how well other people have done in the past, and the meaningfulness or relevance of the task to our self-esteem, well-being, and/or keeping our job. Our expectations are also related to how well someone in a position of authority or supe-riority communicates the desired performance results or possi-ble consequences (either positive or negative) of a perform-ance. There are many times when someone else has a greater influence on our expectations for performance success than we do.[6]

More often than not, though, expectations refer to our per-sonal beliefs about our chances for success rather than some-one else's beliefs. They are intricately linked to our past per-formances and, if past behavior is a predictor of future behav-iors, then our beliefs about future performances should be strongly correlated to the results of previous performances. Quite often, the expectations a performer has about his poten-tial for success will actually predetermine the performance result. Since you become and achieve what you think about most, performers who think about (expect) success succeed more often than not. Those who think about failure most of the time expect to perform poorly, and they usually do. What you think about most and believe the most usually affects your per-ception of reality.

A Story About Expectations

You may have heard this one already, or some variation of it. Now, read it with the mindset that it will give you a clear indication of how managing your expectations determines your behaviors and the results you get.

A traveling salesperson stopped at a farmhouse on a dusty road in what appeared to be the middle of nowhere. The salesperson knocked on the door and the farmer opened it. The salesperson asked the farmer what type of people live in the town down the road. The farmer asked the salesperson what type of people he found in the town he just came from. The salesperson said the people in the town he just left were negative, nasty, and unfriendly. The farmer told the salesperson that he expects the salesperson will find people similar to that in the town up ahead.

A few hours later, another salesperson knocks on the farmer's door, and when the farmer opens it, the salesperson asks the same question. The farmer then asks the salesperson about the people in the town he just came from. This salesperson says the people were friendly, polite, and went out of their way to make him feel comfortable. The farmer tells the salesperson he expects that the people in the town up ahead will be just like that also.

What did the farmer know that psychologist's have tried to prove through years of experimentation? The farmer knew that perceptions, beliefs, and attitudes affect expectations. So when the negative salesperson talked about his previous experiences, the wise farmer knew this person would find what he was "looking for." The same held true for the positive salesperson. We usually get in life what we expect in life. As for performance situations, if we expect to succeed (realistic perceptions, beliefs, and expectations), we will succeed more often than not, and at a higher level. If we expect to fail or perform poorly, we will achieve that goal also because the mind and the body work together to not make a liar out of us. This is the self-fulfilling prophecy. We get what we expect, in life, at work, and during performances. To coin another cliché, it's not that you'll believe it when you see it, but that you'll see it when you believe it. This positive attitude also affects your level of motivation to perform a task.

Vroom[7] described how work or performance motivation is highly influenced by performance expectations. His expectancy theory validates the concept of "believe and achieve" that is depicted so often in popular literature. Another area that performance expectations affect are the results and consequences of that performance. People assign a mental probability to a variety of consequences they may achieve and their perform- ance levels often reflect those ranges. If someone truly believes she will be 100 percent successful and can measure that success, then she will be highly motivated to perform a task. If someone has an expectation that he will only be 50 or 60 percent successful, then he will probably apply a reduced amount of effort to effectively complete a task and achieve the desired result. The attitude or perception is "I really don't have that great a chance to succeed (perform well, win, or what- ever), so why should I put forth my best effort?" Again, the mind and the body work together to make the belief (in this case, the expectation) come true.

Here's another example of the power of expectations. For those of you who remember the original Star Trek television series, the characters often talked about a training simulation at the Star Fleet Academy that no one ever solved (beat). Yet there was one person who did beat (win) the simulation— Captain James T. Kirk. As a television character, Kirk was very competitive, so he went into this simulation expecting to win. When everyone told him that it was never beaten (solved or resolved), Kirk had different ideas. He expected to be suc- cessful, and in order to be successful, he changed the parameters of the situation. Then he beat it. Was he cheating? The show never said as much. All we know is that his expecta- tions for performance success were so high that he found a way to accomplish what no one had ever achieved before. This is another indication of how expectations (in combination with beliefs and attitudes) influence performance results even before someone actually performs.

So the second step in guaranteeing performance improve- ment is to set and clearly communicate performance expecta- tions, and then manage them appropriately based on the per- former's past experiences, past successes, beliefs, attitudes, and knowledge of the rewards and consequences related to the performance. Part of effective expectation management is placing the performer into situations where her skill set is so well matched to the task that it will allow her a greater probability of success. In effect, you are playing to the performer's strengths. This also leads to the concept of talent optimization, which is the next of the seven steps.

Talent Optimization

How do we optimize the skills and strengths of our people so that their potential turns into true performance? How do we get these people to perform at their highest levels possible? If you can answer these questions, you will never be out of work.

There are several effective ways to optimize talent. Training is one approach that is effective to a point. However, there is a point of diminishing returns when a top performer is being trained at a level that is below her capabilities. She already knows the requirements for performance and has achieved the expected objectives, yet she has to attend the training class with her colleagues so that "everyone is on the same page." While this may be a way to start to optimize talent for some people, you are actually sub-optimizing the talent of the top performer. That's because she will become bored, lose focus, and probably allow her performance to "regress to the mean." She will become more like the average performers in the group instead of remaining at the top.

If you decide that training is one way to optimize performance, take the time to individualize and customize the training so that it meets the requirements of each particular performer. One way to do this is to identify the performer's strengths, and focus on enhancing those strengths. Books published by the Gallup organization support the strengths approach to talent optimization.[8] Anecdotal evidence will give you the same result. Ask any performer what she would like to hear more about, her strengths or her weaknesses, and she will tell you her strengths. Most people know when they do something wrong or perform poorly. They don't have to be reminded about it or constantly told about it. They would rather focus on their strengths because they believe that if you enhance the strengths, the weaknesses will automatically improve since they will eventually be performing at an even higher level.

Another model that supports this concept of talent optimization is Positive CORE. CORE stands for the four elements that will always lead to positive performance improvement when they are applied to an individual performer.[9] These elements are **C**onfidence, **O**utcomes, **R**elationships, and **E**ngagement. (Please note that the term *Outcomes* is used here in the same way *results* has been used throughout the book. The CORE model requires the use of Outcomes to make the acronym work, even though its use conflicts slightly with the definitions provided by Kaufman in his OEM model.)

Confidence refers to how a performer feels about himself, his strengths and talents, what types of reinforcements or consequences he will receive for a performance, and his belief in himself as a performer. Outcomes refer to the goals and objectives a person sets for a performance, his expectations of successfully achieving those objectives, how his performance will be measured in relation to others and to his previous performances, and how the results he achieves affect himself, his team, his organization, and society. Relationships are all about how well a person gets along with people, including a manager, colleagues, friends, and family, and with other social contacts. The old adage in sales that people buy from people they like can be transferred to performance to say that people perform better with and for people they like to be with. Engagement involves the commitment level of the performer, his emotions and arousal states relative to each performance, and his level of optimism, which also ties back to his confidence and belief in himself. These four elements that make up the CORE are critical to optimizing talent and guaranteeing performance improvement.

If you doubt the efficacy and power of this approach, and I can't see how you can, ask yourself this: If someone has little to no self-confidence, is unclear about the desired results, has a poor or no relationship with others he works with, and lacks the motivation to perform, can he ever be a top performer? When a person lacks these CORE elements, you can be sure that no appreciable performance improvement will occur. When a person possesses these CORE elements, you can guarantee performance improvement will occur.

Recognition

Everyone loves to be recognized. You know this is true by watching a person light up when you call their name, or turn around when they hear their name mentioned. You also see the opposite reaction when you see someone you've met before, but you can't remember their name. They remember your name, but you stare at them with a blank look, and they more likely than not get their feelings hurt. They, like you, long to be recognized. Recognition—along with its sibling, appreciation—is probably the number one human desire of all time.

People on the job feel exactly the same way. They want to be recognized for their work and their contributions. They want to know that what they do has an impact beyond just where they are working. Some people want financial recognition for what they accomplish, and others want visual recognition like plaques and certificates. Some people may want other forms of tangible recognition, while many people are satisfied with a simple thank you or a pat on the back.

Young children are very literal in their interpretations of language. A story I mentioned earlier in the book briefly bears repeating. Years ago, I learned the difference between verbal recognition (a spoken "pat on the back") and physical recognition (a literal pat on the back). My son made a good play in a baseball game, and afterward, I told him I was proud of him. He looked a little sad and I asked him why, since I just gave him a pat on the back. He said that I only *told* him I was proud of him, but I didn't give him a *real* pat on the back. He wanted actual physical recognition for his accomplishment. The lesson here is that people want to be recognized in ways that are significant and meaningful to them. Some want visual, others want verbal, and still others want physical recognition. There are some who want money, and others who want time with their families. Whatever their preferred method of recognition, we learn two things here. The first is that everyone wants to feel appreciated. The other is that recognition—preferably positive but sometimes even negative—provides feedback and validation that helps us build and maintain our self-esteem and often increases our self-confidence. Now, you may ask how negative recognition can lead to performance improvement. The best example is from sports. There are many athletes who thrive on the coach fussing and yelling at them. It motivates them for some reason. Even though the coach's behavior can be viewed as negative, the athlete perceives it as a form of recognition and responds by performing better—in a positive manner. So if you want to guarantee performance improvement, ask your performers how they want to be recognized.

Imagination

I am using the term *imagination* to also include *imagery* and *visualization*. Experience has taught us a few things about the power of the imagination. For example, in a "contest" between the will and the imagination, the imagination will always win out. Could it be that the subconscious mind (the imagination) is stronger than the conscious mind (the will)? It has been said that the mind does not know the difference between a real and an imagined event. This means that what we actually see and what we see in our mind's eye (our imagination) create the same or similar responses, perceptions, and memories.

Furthermore, the positive and beneficial effects of imagery/visualization have been documented in sports, health-care, public speaking, surgery, hypnosis, test taking, dancing, video gaming, and a host of other areas. For example, I let my imagination run wild in a variety of settings: before I give a speech, prior to conducting a training program, before playing a sport, and before writing this section of the book. I envision a successful result in my mind first and then my mind and body go out to make it a reality.

Our greatest inventions and discoveries are due to someone's imagination—that person's ability to see something in their mind before making it a reality. For example, the telephone, the light bulb, the automobile, the Internet, laptop computers, cell phones, and almost anything else you can name came from someone's imagination. So in order to use this powerful tool to help guarantee performance improvement, teach your people to relax, practice their task in their minds as if they were doing it perfectly for real, and then repeat the process. The more you can visualize a successful achievement in your mind, the greater the probability that you will actually realize that achievement. When you use mental imagery to rehearse a performance first before actually doing it, when you do it, it's like déjà vu all over again. You've already been there, done that. The performance comes easier and usually at a higher level. The power of imagination once again elevates performance. Imagine the possibilities.[10]

Concentration

Along with imagining success, you have to be able to concentrate on your desired results. You must focus your attention so that nothing distracts you. Top performers in all fields talk about being in the zone—in a state of flow. They are so focused on their task and the result they want to achieve that nothing breaks that concentration. Sometimes, when they are concentrating so hard or are locked into this high performance zone, they achieve a state of perceptual blindness. This is where nothing can interfere with what they are concentrating on—not noise, visual stimuli, environmental changes, nothing. They are so focused and locked in that their attention cannot be diverted.

Concentration helps improve performance because it does not allow you to be distracted by extraneous or external cues. Think of a basketball player shooting a foul shot and the home crowd waving things behind the basket. The player has to block out all that visual stimuli as well as the crowd noise to make the shot. The player must focus her concentration to such a fine point that nothing will get in the way. The second the player starts to think about the shot or anything else that is going on, there is a great chance she will miss. So the advice is to concentrate and do, but don't think too much.

Also, you shouldn't concentrate too hard. We all have heard stories of people who say they were concentrating so hard on something that their head started to hurt. You can actually physically tense your muscles to create that headache if you "think too hard." The key to successful concentration and high performance is to achieve a state of relaxed alertness.

This is when you can take in all the appropriate stimuli and weed out the inappropriate distractions. It is also the mental state that lets you properly perceive everything around you so that things seem to move in slow motion. People who achieve this mental flow or zone state talk about things moving in slow motion, or the baseball being so easy to hit because it looked like the size of a bowling ball, or any other number of descriptions where time apparently stands still. You can get into this prime state of concentration by relaxing in a manner similar to what you would use for imagination and visualization, then becoming aware of what you want to focus on and directing all your attention on that object without allowing any distractions to occur. Your performances will soar when you can concentrate during your mental imagery practice.

Habituation

Habituation for our purposes means making something a habit—you do it so much that it becomes a natural part of your behavior. Instead of habituating yourself to something to the point of it becoming rote, I'm suggesting we accept the term to mean that you create a long-term habit for your performance. Some professionals might even call it ritualization, which is a series of behaviors or actions a person does each time before he or she performs something.

This habit formation occurs when you engage in repetitive, perfect practice. There is no sense in practicing to make mistakes. You want to practice perfectly because you want to perform perfectly, and you want to ingrain all these patterns into your brain, your neuromuscular system, and your behavioral repertoire. Remember that perfect practice prevents poor performance. Do it right the first time, do it right every time you practice, and you'll do it right when you perform it for real. The habit becomes ingrained and it occurs naturally. To use a computer analogy, you have created a program (in this case of performance, you have created a motor program) that once initiated, runs automatically and perfectly to completion. You do not have to interfere with it. No conscious intervention is required because you are habituated to performing well. You know what to do and how to do it. In fact, the performance itself may become so habitual that it resembles a ritual, which is something you do every time in the same way without even thinking about it. Many performers have their own pre-performance rituals that lead right into their high level performance habits. The pre-performance rituals are actually the trigger portion of the habitual performance pattern. In fact, because of my background in sport and performance psychology, I have been able to help clients identify the sequential steps in their performance patterns, determine which steps occur habitually and which do not, and then work on the nonhabitual steps to integrate them into a whole performance pattern that "fires off automatically" because it has now become a habit.

GET RICH to Guarantee Performance Improvement

There you have it: the GET RICH approach to guaranteeing performance improvement. Although some may say the mnemonic is a little self-serving (it really is my e-mail address), please remember that it is easy to remember and it fits in your memory. Plus, it gives you an easy model to follow for performance improvement.

If one part of the GET RICH approach is off, you can go in and work on that area. Find out which, if any, of these seven areas is preventing someone from achieving a high level of performance. Then identify their strengths in that area, even if their performance is below desired levels. Remember that everyone has strengths when they perform. You will just have to find them. After you find the strengths, work to enhance them in the given area and you'll see the weakness disappear. The end result will be performance improvement. Like the television commercial says, "I guarantee it."

Endnotes

1. Gerson, R. F., & Gerson, R. G., (2006). *Positive performance improvement: A new paradigm for optimizing your workforce.* Palo Alto, CA: Davies-Black.

2. Kaufman, R., Oakley-Browne, H., Watkins, R., & Leigh, D., (2003). *Strategic planning for success: Aligning people, performance and payoffs.* San Francisco, CA: Jossey-Bass. See also Kaufman, R., (2006). *Change, choice and consequences.* Amherst, MA: HRD Press.

3. The concept of BHAG was introduced in several publications at various times, and most notably by J. Collins & J. Porras in *Built to Last* (New York: HarperBusiness, 1994). The BHAG is very similar to the stretch goals. The concept is designed to get people to stretch beyond what they originally thought they were capable of achieving.

4. This is just another approach to motivate people to perform beyond their perceived capabilities and expectations. Usually, when you get people to commit to what they previously thought was an "unreachable star," they find a way to "achieve the impossible dream." You will also find this approach used in P. Georgescu's (2005), *The Source of Success* (San Francisco, CA: Jossey-Bass).

5. See, for example, Branden, N., (1995). *Six pillars of self-esteem.* New York: Bantam Books, and Kanter, R. M., (2004). *Confidence: How winning streaks and losing streaks begin and end.* (New York: Crown Business).

6. We see this in the notion of the Little League parent or stage parent. This parent pushes the child incessantly and excessively to perform at ever-increasing levels. The child may somehow live up to the task and expectations, and then the parent is happy. More often than not, the overbearing parent causes the child to withdraw from the activity and lose their intrinsic motivation to perform the activity. Since most of us have experienced something like this in our lives, we can easily make the leap to the workplace and substitute employee for child and manager for parent. The manager has excessively high expectations about

what we should be accomplishing and we feel it is out of our reach. Even if we enjoyed the task at one time, we will lose our motivation for it because of the "pounding" the manager puts on us to reach those unreachable (in the performer's mind) levels of performance.

7. Vroom, V., (1994). *Work and motivation.* San Francisco, CA: Jossey-Bass.

8. Several books by the Gallup organization, including M. Buckingham's and C. Coffman's *First, Break All the Rules,* (New York: Simon & Schuster, 1999) and M. Buckingham's *The One Thing You Need to Know,* (New York: Free Press, 2005), along with M. Buckingham's and D. Clifton's *Now, Discover Your Strengths* (New York: Free Press, 2001) and B. Smith's and T. Rutiglioano's *Discover Your Sales Strengths* (New York: Warner, 2003), focus on the power of playing to people's strengths as a way to either improve performance or consistently achieve high levels of performance.

9. Gerson, R. F., & Gerson, R. G., (2006). *Positive performance improvement: A new paradigm for optimizing your workforce.* Palo Alto, CA: Davies-Black.

10. You will find some visualization and imagery scripts in these books: Gerson, R., (2004). *HEADcoaching: Mental training for peak performance.* Bloomington, IN: Authorhouse; Loehr, J., (1986). *Mental toughness training for sports.* New York: Penguin; Ungerleider, S., (2005). *Mental training for peak performance: Top athletes reveal the mind exercises they use to excel.* PA: Rodale; and Kuehl, K., et al. (2005). *Mental toughness: A champion's state of mind.* Chicago: Ivan Dee.

Chapter 5
Managing Stress and Guaranteeing Performance Improvement

Imagine you are playing in the NCAA basketball championship game. Your team is down one point, you get fouled and have two free throws, and there is one second on the clock. What are you thinking? What are you feeling? What are you telling yourself to do?

Or picture yourself playing in the Masters golf championship. You are on the 18th green, putting for a birdie that will give you a win over Tiger Woods. Your ball is only three feet from the cup. This should be a "gimmee." If it was match play, they probably would concede the putt to you. But this is the Masters, and it is the final hole, and you are one putt away from beating the best golfer in the world. What are you thinking? What are you feeling? What are you telling yourself? Are your hands sweaty? Are your knees shaking? Are you having trouble breathing? Is your mind racing? Or, are you cool, calm, collected, and relaxed?

You can be any or all of these things, almost at the same time. Stress, and the accompanying pressure of performing in front of a crowd or with something important on the line, has a tremendous effect on performance. We all feel it. We all know what stress is. And each of us reacts in our own special way to stress. Some people thrive on it. Others do whatever they can just to survive. Still others collapse under the pressure, curl up in a fetal position, or take their ball and go home. Whatever metaphor you want to use to describe the negative effects of stress on performance, you know that two things happen: Performance deteriorates and any hopes of improving performance go down the tubes with it as your inability to handle the pressure increases.

So the question becomes how do we manage stress so that we can improve performance, guarantee that improvement, and ultimately thrive under pressure? This chapter will provide you with some suggestions to make stress your ally and to develop the ability to achieve peak performance, virtu-ally on demand. But first, let's talk about a precursor to stress episodes. That precursor is burnout.

Preventing Burnout and Improving Performance

The best analogy for what burnout is in the human body is an electrical brownout in a city. Basically, the power is still there, but the effective use of that power is not. During a brownout, everything is reduced. The electrical power is reduced, the speed with which people move or accomplish things is reduced (possibly because of the darkness), and the feelings of control are reduced (you know this is happening because people are constantly asking others when the power will come back on). During burnout, you experience similar things. Your energy level is reduced, your effort and achievements are lower, and you feel that you have little or no control of your situations. Burnout is very much like a grey cloud hanging over you, and you get a feeling of malaise. You're not totally out of it, but you are not totally with it either. The burnout most often starts out psychological and moves to becoming physiological. So what can we do about it?

The first thing is to understand what causes burnout in any performer. Most jobs are fast-paced (which can produce high stress), while there are others that can become very repetitive. Continuous repetition without change or the chance for change leads to boredom (and sometimes, anxiety). These situations can cause negative feelings as well as stress. However, before the stress becomes full-blown, you experience burnout first. You now must find some sort of release. Without a release for these negative feelings, performers experience burnout.

Burnout is the feeling that precedes a full-blown stress attack. When you're burned out, you've just had enough of whatever you are doing. You are slightly depressed, lethargic, unmotivated, possibly confused or at least not thinking clearly, and you may experience some physical symptoms. Basically, you just can't take it anymore and want to run away and hide (or curl up in a fetal position).

If you're experiencing a visible reduction in performance or productivity from yourself or your people, consider that they, or you, might be suffering from varying degrees of burnout. **Here is how to turn them from meek performers into peak performers.**

Realize that burnout has both physical and psychological symptoms and causes. Physically, you can change the layout of the workplace, the seating arrangements, the chairs themselves, the lighting, the temperature, the noise levels, and anything else in the work environment that might be detracting from performance. Sometimes physical changes in the environment or just getting people to move about results in improved performance. Sometimes, but not always. That's because burnout has a psychological component that is very powerful.

Psychologically, you have to do many more things. You have to understand the causes of each person's burnout, why they feel that way, and what you can do to decrease or prevent their burnout in order to increase their performance.

To beat burnout, CHARGE your people up.

Challenge them as much as you can. People have to be challenged to be motivated. We all want to achieve something, and a challenge provides that brass ring to strive for. You can challenge your employees with sales or service goals, incentives, competitions, contests, or anything else that they find motivating. Challenge them to make the organization better, to achieve at levels that will become their personal bests, and to help their customers' customers be successful. People love a challenge, and they usually rise to the occasion.

Help them develop the trait of **Hardiness**. Hardiness refers to the psychological ability to bounce back from stress and other negative situations. It is a form of psychological resilience. Resilience is critical to performing under pressure. It is what makes some performers welcome adversity. Resilient people sometimes even look for stressful situations because they know that they will be tested and that they will pass the test. Performers who possess hardiness and resilience will shrug off a bad situation and then will, for example, provide great service or make a big sale on the next call.

Appreciation is the most basic desire of all human beings. Show your people that you appreciate their efforts. Recognize what they do and how well they do it on a regular basis. Say thank you to them, congratulate them on a job well done, and just let them know you appreciate all the work they do for the company and its customers. Employees who are appreciated, recognized, and respected will perform better in all situations, especially under pressure.

Relax. When you consider the fast pace of most jobs today and the number of customers or tasks each person must handle, there never seems to be enough time to do it all. That's when burnout and stress start to occur. The key, here, is that there must be time for relaxation. Everyone has to have a break, and not just their scheduled break. Allow employees to leave their desks, stretch out, walk around, and talk to other people. Allow them to perform tasks that are not typically within their job responsibilities. Ideally, create a quiet room where people can go, sit down, close their eyes, forget the pressures of the day, and just relax. This will go a long way to preventing burnout and improving performance, especially since burnout/stress and relaxation cannot coexist (more about this later when we talk about relaxation).[1]

Set **G**oals with the employees. Have them write down measurable goals that are somewhat difficult to achieve. This goes along with the first suggestion of challenging the staff to perform well. People who set and achieve goals handle stress more effectively and are generally more satisfied with their personal and work lives than those who don't. Then help them set true performance objectives. (We talked about this earlier in the book in the section on goal setting.) True, measurable performance objectives will help people stay focused on their tasks, work hard to achieve their desired results, and perform in such a way that they will be appreciated and recognized.

Show **E**mpathy. Being any type of performer in today's fast-paced world is a tough job. Sometimes, people just require someone to listen to them and to show them they care. Empathy helps performers overcome the stress of the job and prevent burnout. Just having someone who listens and understands how they feel makes people want to return to work and achieve more. Empathy from managers will also strengthen the relationship between them and their performers, and we know that a strong relationship leads to improved performance. People just want to do better for managers they like.

That is the way to **CHARGE** up your people to prevent burnout and perform well under pressure. One other idea is to **provide nutritious snacks and plenty of water** if food is allowed in your offices or wherever the performance takes place. The more water your people drink and the more nutritiously they eat, the more nourished their brains will be. This will make them better able to handle stress and reduce the possibility of burnout. The result of all these suggestions will be a drop in burnout and a boom in performance.[2]

Improving Performance Through Rest, Relaxation, and Recovery

Ask any performer how they can get better at what they do, and they will all tell you basically the same thing. They say they have to train more, work harder, get in better shape (if their performance is physical), practice their skills more often, gain more consistency, and the list goes on and on. All these things are true, and they will help every performer improve.

But performers who follow this approach leave out some important elements for performance improvement. The first is that they neglect to practice the psychological and mental skills as much as they practice their physical skills. I have talked about the importance of mental training throughout this book and elsewhere.[3] In addition to physical and mental training, there are also three skills that will be described below that actually help you perform better in all situations throughout your life. They are **rest, relaxation,** and **recovery**.

The Best of Rest

Everyone agrees that rest is important. After all, we sleep at night, take naps when we're tired, and just plain old crash when we do not have any energy left. Yet while we agree that rest is important and we all realize we must rest, most people never seem to get enough rest. In fact, research shows that adults require 7 to 8 hours of sleep a night and children sometimes require even more. Yet most people only get 4 to 6 hours of sleep a night. We have become a nation of overachievers and under-sleepers. **If we want to be the best, we have to get more rest**. This is especially true in the time-crunched lifestyles that we lead, with so much time being devoted to "work" and not enough time being devoted to leisure, recreation, exercise, and rest. It is as if we have to squeeze in what is best for us.

Picture yourself in a competitive sporting event. It can be an individual sport like golf, tennis, or running, or a team sport like basketball, baseball, or softball. You've already done all your physical training and practice. The night before the big match or game, you know instinctively that you should save your energy and get *enough* rest. This way you will be fresh for the competition. Unfortunately, your mind is usually racing with thoughts about the big game and you tend to sleep poorly. Even when you try to rest without sleeping, you are unable to do it. You constantly toss and turn and practically wear yourself out.

Now picture yourself having to make a big presentation that will affect your future work. Again, it's the night before and you're trying to get enough sleep so that you'll be rested and energized the next day for your presentation. But something is going on in your head. You keep thinking about the presentation and all the "what ifs" that might happen to make it go bad. You keep worrying and worrying that you'll never fall asleep, and you don't. And when you do, it is not a very restful sleep. In fact, you may toss and turn all night because of the stress. In this case, as in the sports example, stress prevents rest.

The problem is that **you are trying to rest.** You are forcing yourself to rest, and your mind and body are rebelling. It is just like with anything else in life. The harder you try to do some thing, the more difficult it actually becomes to do it. For example, think of a performance you had to give where you worked yourself up into a frenzy about doing well. You got yourself over-hyped and over-motivated. You were so pumped up that you became anxious and tense. Your arousal level, to use a psychological term, was way too high. And when this happens, performance suffers. In fact, when your arousal level is too high or too low, you rarely perform at your best. That is also why you cannot fall asleep and get enough rest.

When I work with athletes and executives, I give them this advice on how to get an appropriate amount of rest. First, they must maintain their regular schedule of sleeping, eating, exercising, and performing. If regular exercise or activity is part of their daily routine, I tell them to maintain that schedule wherever they are. Whenever you change your habitual activities and/or disrupt your body clock, rest becomes difficult. Even if you are traveling across time zones, try to maintain your regular schedule. I know when I fly from Florida to California to make a speech or conduct a seminar, I do everything I can to stay on Eastern time. That is because my trips are usually only for two or three days, and I know I will perform better if I eat, sleep, rest, and exercise on my regular schedule. So keep your regular schedule.

The next thing I recommend is that they do something to make their eyes "heavy." This can be reading a book, watching television too long, or even staring up at one spot on the ceiling. When your eyes get heavy, just close them naturally, and you will fall into a *restful* sleep. This nap (or even better, a full night's sleep) will allow you to awaken feeling refreshed.

The third thing I tell them to do is to remove themselves from all stressful situations, if possible. Some people take a warm bath, others get a massage. Some people do yoga, while others simply stretch. Whatever method or technique you would use to remove yourself from a stressful situation or to turn off your mind, just do it. This way, your mind and body can **rest by relaxing.** When someone is relaxed, it is physiologically and psychologically impossible for them to become stressed out, therefore, they rest naturally.

Relax, Don't Sweat It

Relaxation is crucial to everyone's well-being. The more active you are, the more you require relaxation to counterbalance your life. Also, too much stress in your life causes stress hormones to run wild through your body. And even if you think you're over the stress, the hormones are still doing their damage. For example, if you've ever come close to having a car accident, you'll remember how you did everything you could to avoid the accident, and then after you successfully avoided the collision, you continued driving. No more stress, right? Wrong! A few seconds, or even a few minutes, later, those stress hormones flood your body and you start to feel anxious and nervous, even though there was no accident and little chance of something else happening. Also, the more negative your attitude is toward your life, your job, your sport, your family, or things in general, the more stressed out you become (and maybe even angry or depressed). One of the best ways to overcome this negative state is to relax.

Relaxation has so many health and performance benefits that I cannot even list them all. Some of them include more energy to perform, better focus and attention on your tasks, easier and deeper breathing, less muscle tension and physical mistakes, better and clearer decision making, better coordination, less mental interference with your performance, better relationships with people, and a higher self-esteem.

Relaxation can often be accompanied by positive affirmations and visualization. I help people develop these positive statements about themselves and then create pictures in their minds of great performances. Using relaxation techniques, I have helped executives calm their fears about giving a speech in public, as well as meeting new people. Salespeople have also increased their closing ratios because they are more relaxed and do not give off nervous signals when they make a sales presentation. Managers who were taught to relax found themselves better able to deliver performance evaluations to employees, especially if the evaluations were not that positive. The bottom line is this: Relaxation and stress or tension can never co-exist because they are direct opposites in the mind and body. So if you find yourself getting too tense, too stressed out, too anxious, or too angry, learn to relax and watch your performance improve.

For example, a 62-year-old female golfer I worked with lowered her handicap 5 strokes just by using relaxation and visualization. A 23-year-old male golfer who was on the early satellite tours never placed high enough to cash in. After several mental training sessions that involved deep breathing, relaxation, and visualization, he cashed in four tournaments in a row. A 36-year-old male tennis player had trouble getting his second serve in with any velocity because he was scared (too tense) he would double fault. We worked together using relaxation, visualization, and affirmations to help him gain confidence in his second serve so that he would not lay it up there for his opponent. His second serve began landing in the service box and became almost as fast as his first serve.

A salesperson I worked with froze when she had to make a presentation to a group larger than five people. We used a variety of relaxation techniques to calm her down and then used visualization to help her mentally rehearse the presentation in front of large groups. After several practice sessions, she was able to make her presentation effortlessly and flawlessly, regardless of how many people were in the audience. Another example: A rising female executive had difficulty telling her male counterparts when she disagreed with them. By using deep breathing as a relaxation exercise, she was able to go into meetings calmer than before, keep her attention focused on her task of promoting her position on an issue, and handle any questions or objections to her position that came her way. And she was able to professionally disagree with her male colleagues. As a result of acquiring this skill, she improved her overall job performance.

If you are an avid runner, you know the importance of stretching out both before and after you run. Stretching is a form of relaxation because a stretched (relaxed) muscle cannot be tense. Relaxation can be considered mental stretching. When you combine mental and physical relaxation with muscle stretching, you provide multiple benefits for your mind and body. In addition, you'll have more energy to perform your activity.

The best and quickest way to relax is to take five to seven slow, deep breaths. Count to 8 as you inhale, and 8 again as you exhale. Focus on your breathing and concentrate on taking in as much air as you can. Then, when you exhale, focus on "blowing the tension right out of your body." This imagery will lead to a relaxed state for you.

Another approach to relaxation is to alternately tense and then relax specific muscle groups. By doing this, you learn the difference between how you feel when you are stressed out and when you are relaxed. Some people never learn this difference, so they live in a state of muscular tension all their lives. This will also lead to high blood pressure, cardiac diseases, and possibly stroke. **So relax, don't sweat it**. Use these techniques while you are alone in a quiet place as well as when you are preparing to give a major presentation, to complete a job requirement, or to play a sport. You will find that your performances, in all areas of your life, will improve.

The Road to Recovery

Recovery is a phenomenon that few people pay attention to and even fewer know about. It is the time between your actual performance and your next performance. It is a time when you can "recover" from the stress of what you were doing and properly prepare for what you have to do next. In tennis, it is the time between points or games. In golf, it is the time between shots. In weightlifting, it is the time between sets. In making a presentation, it can be the time between changing the slides (you have to recover quickly in this situation) or moving from one topic to another. Recovery is the in-between time when your mind and body have a chance to relax and "return to normal," or to a higher state of normalcy, depending on what you are doing.[4]

Many times, whether it is in sports, on the job, or when we're learning a new task, we work on something, make progress, and then reach a plateau. When we are at this point, it seems that no matter what we do, we cannot improve. We might try harder, work longer, or do something different. We push ourselves to get better. Yet nothing seems to work, and we stay "stuck" at the same level. That is because your body is going through a **prolonged state of recovery**. It is getting itself together, so to speak, to take you to the next level. This means you have to give it time to recover. Be patient and don't rush it. Use the plateau as a learning experience. In psychology, performance plateaus are often called consolidation periods, where everything we've done and learned about a task up to this specific point in time is being consolidated into a cohesive behavior. Over time, this combined, cohesive behavior will become automatic, and you will easily perform at a higher level.

It is up to you to use this analogy when you are involved in any task. Use the in-between time to prepare yourself for your next effort. For example, after you hit a poor shot in golf (and we all do), don't stand around cursing yourself or complaining about how bad the shot was. There is nothing you can do about it once it leaves the club head. It is over. So you can either spend your post-shot time (recovery period) worrying and fretting about the past, which will probably mess up your next shot, or you can positively prepare yourself for the next shot. How many times have you seen a professional golfer hit a terrible shot off the tee only to recover on the next shot or two to make birdie or par? Or how many times have you seen professional tennis players play a poor point, and then come back on the next point or in the next game to play like the champions they are? And how many times have you seen a professional speaker lose the audience on one topic and quickly recover to win them back on the next topic?

They can do this because they have mastered their recovery periods and are able to use them wisely. Here is an analogy that should help you. When you lift weights, you usually work out every other day. This is so your muscles can rest and *recover* from the workout. Remember that your strength gains come during recovery periods, not during your weightlifting activities. If you were to lift weights every day, you would eventually become fatigued more easily and weaker because you were not giving your body a chance to recover. So, in weightlifting, the off day in addition to your between-sets time make up your recovery period.

In golf or tennis, or basketball or baseball, the time in between activity is your recovery period. The same is true for a sales call or a business meeting. When it's over, just review it for what it was. Consider the facts about what happened and learn from it. This is your business recovery period.

You can enhance your recovery by doing some physical as well as mental exercises during this time. I recommend that everyone breathe deeply, relax, visualize their next great performance, and recite positive affirmations to themselves. As unscientific as this may sound, it works. We know it works because many researchers in the field of sports psychology and positive psychology have tested these concepts and approaches with athletes and performers at all skill levels, and they always get the same results.[5]

What you do during your recovery period **has a direct effect on your next performance.**

Recognizing the Signs of Stress that Affect Performance

Now that you know what to do about stress and how it affects performance, here are some signs that will help you recognize if you are under stress. These signs relate to the negative effects of stress. (There are positive signs and positive effects of stress, which will be discussed in the next section.) Remember that not everyone experiences all these signs, but many of us experience a significant number of them. Signs of stress can manifest themselves as physical, emotional, or relational. If any of these signs or symptoms appear for too long a period of time, you could be making yourself ill. The one thing we can guarantee is that prolonged exposure to stress will definitely hurt your performance in any area. Here are some of, but not all of, the signs and symptoms:[6]

Physical symptoms

- Sleep disturbances
- Back, shoulder, or neck pain
- Tension or migraine headaches
- Stomach problems
- Weight gain or loss; eating disorders
- Muscle tension or muscle weakness
- Fatigue
- Irregular heartbeat, palpitations, or chest pain
- Shortness of breath
- Sweaty palms or hands, or cold hands or feet
- Immune system suppression: more colds, flu, infections
- High blood pressure

Emotional symptoms

- Nervousness, anxiety, tension
- Easy to anger or excessive anger, irritability, frustration
- Lowered self-esteem and self-confidence, possible victim mentality
- Depression, moodiness
- "Butterflies"
- Memory problems
- Trouble thinking clearly or misperceiving situations or events
- Feeling out of control
- Lack of responsibility for actions; blaming others
- Phobias or irrational fears
- Overreactions
- Lack of concentration; inability to focus

Relational symptoms

- Increased arguments
- Isolation from social activities; social withdrawal
- Conflict with co-workers or employers; lack of cooperative behaviors
- Frequent job changes
- Decreased communication
- Lack of physical contact with significant others
- Domestic or workplace violence
- Overreactions

Stress can also come from your own:

- Irresponsible or irrational behavior
- Poor health habits
- Negative attitudes and feelings toward self and others
- Unrealistic or poorly communicated expectations
- Perfectionism and/or fear of making mistakes
- The disease to please
- Poor relationships with your boss

Not All Stress is Bad

For the most part, stress and its relationship to performance have gotten a bad rap. Everyone thinks that stress is bad for you, it harms you, and it always detracts from your performance. While this can happen some of the time, it does not happen all the time. There really is a good type of stress. It is called eustress, and it is a contraction of the words *euphoric* and *stress.* Where negative stress or distress can hurt you, eustress is positive stress. It is the kind of stress that makes you feel good, that makes you perform at a higher level, and that helps you get into that flow state or optimal performance zone. Eustress is what top performers crave because they turn it into a peak performance. If you look back at the list of the negative signs of stress, you'll notice that one of them says "butterflies." We have all felt the butterflies in our stomachs, the extra nervous energy, and even the pain that sometimes goes with it. Even with eustress, you still get the butterflies. You just make sure they are flying in formation and in the right direction. Here's a little secret about eustress and top performers:" All top performers get a little nervous before they "go on." It is only natural, and top performers do whatever it takes to generate that nervous energy. Where they separate themselves from ordinary performers is that top performers channel that energy properly and make sure the butterflies are flying in formation. So next time you feel yourself getting overwhelmed before a performance, and you think that the negative stress is going to get to you, remember what peak performers do.

Recommendations for Peak Performance

Here are seven suggestions for you to manage your stress and become a peak performer on demand—using stress to generate a great performance whenever necessary.

1. Get enough rest by keeping on a regular schedule, including eating, sleeping, exercising, and doing your job (e.g., playing sports).

2. When you find your energy levels low, and you have enough time before a performance, engage in something that will make your eyes heavy and cause you to relax and rest. This will help you "recharge your batteries."

3. Practice relaxation exercises several times every day. Balance activity with rest and relaxation. The mental and physical benefits of this "workout" will permeate all aspects of your life, including physical and mental performance and health.

4. Use your recovery periods to prepare yourself for your next performance.

5. Say positive things to yourself at all times. These are known as positive affirmations.

6.   Imagine yourself always performing well. This will build your self-esteem and your self-confidence, and help you overcome the negative signs, symptoms, and effects of stress.

7.   Always remember the true power of rest, relaxation, and recovery to help you be a top performer and guarantee performance improvement in most situations.

Endnotes

1.   Herbert Benson has been a pioneer in this field for many years. His first book on the subject, *The Relaxation Response* (New York: HarperTorch, 1976—reissue) was followed by *Beyond the Relaxation Response* (CA: Berkeley, 1985). More recently, he applied these principles to high performance in H. Benson's & W. Proctor's, *The Breakout Principle* (New York: Simon & Schuster, 2004).

2.   We see this being done more and more with athletes in all sports. Frequent water breaks and small, nutritional snacks help athletes keep their energy levels up, which results in higher and sustained performance. For more on this, see Gerson, R., (2004). *HEADcoaching: Mental training for peak performance.* Bloomington, IN: Authorhouse; Loehr, J., & Schwartz, T., *The power of full engagement.* New York: Free Press; and Groppel, J., (1999). *The corporate athlete.* New York: John Wiley.

3.   See the Gerson reference for *HEADcoaching,* in Note 2 as well as Gerson, R., (2006). *Achieving high performance: A research-based practical approach.* Amherst, MA: HRD Press.

4.   Jim Loehr has done a great deal of work in the area of recovery and high performance. His original work was with athletes, and then he extended the research to business people. The results were the same. People who could recover faster (come down from high stress or anxiety levels) usually performed better, won contests or events more often, and felt better about themselves and their performances.

5.   See the Gerson reference above as well as Seligman, M., (2002). *Authentic happiness.* New York: Free Press; and Kanter, R. M., (2004). *Confidence: How winning streaks and losing streaks begin and end.* New York: Crown Business.

6.   There are literally thousands of resources on stress and its symptoms. One suggestion is for the reader to put stress symptoms into any search engine and review the lists that are presented on the various sites. A word of caution to hypochondriacs: Just because you are reading this list or any other list of stress symptoms does not mean you have them or will get them. The lists are for educational and awareness purposes only. Also, if you've ever taken a stress management workshop, your participant manual will have a list of symptoms that you can use for identification purposes.

Chapter 6
Because Results Matter

Several years ago, some parents came to me because their son was underperforming in school. Specifically, he was having trouble with fourth-grade math. The teacher said it was because he didn't possess basic math skills and all the tutoring that had been done up to that point had not "brought him up to speed." The parents contacted me as a last resort because the school was about to keep their son back. This bothered them for two reasons. The first was that he wouldn't be moving on with his friends and the second was that he was the tallest boy in the class, so if he was held back, he'd be even taller than the other students and possibly become a social outcast.

As you will learn throughout this chapter, there are numerous things you can do to achieve performance improvement, and then when you get "good enough" and confident enough, you can actually guarantee that you will achieve performance improvement. The problem in the industry is that we are locked into formulas, theories, models, flow charts, and doing research, and we forget about our ultimate result: the achievement of measurable and sustainable results. If we can't guarantee that we can achieve those results, why should anyone work with us? It is not enough to conduct the research in the field and get statistically valid results. We have to develop tools and techniques so that the research can be put to practical use and everyone who uses these techniques feels so confident that they will guarantee positive results.

The parents heard me say this on a television show and that is why they called me. I interviewed their son and found out what he liked and disliked about school, about his teacher, about math, and about sports. You see, he was an excellent soccer player. In fact, he was the top player on his youth sports team. So I took him out to a soccer field and watched a change come over him. Instead of being downtrodden and upset that he was not smart, was no good, and couldn't "get the job done," he transformed into a highly confident child who believed he could accomplish anything. He was in his element.

Seeing this, I asked him how he felt playing soccer. He said he felt "magical." His favorite position was goalie because he totally controlled the result of the game. So we went to the goal and started talking about the soccer field.

We talked about how long the field was, how long the goalie box was (both length and width), and how far he could kick a ball. We discussed kicking a ball to mid-field and he did the math in his head to tell me the yardage. We went through a series of "math problems" like this and he calculated (added, subtracted, divided, and multiplied) all things soccer and field related in his head. We then went back to his house and used the soccer field as his metaphorical math environment. We were playing to his strengths in a positive environment where he felt confident, knew the results that were expected of him, was comfortable in our relationship as coach and player (counselor and student), and was committed to succeed. As long as these four parameters were in place,[1] he could successfully complete his math problems. So I provided this information to his teacher and with a little bit of individualized instruction, this child was able to catch up and do math on his grade level and get promoted with his class.

The funny thing is that I never tutored him in math. I guaranteed his parents I could help him learn more effectively and improve his math performance. But I never taught him how to do his math problems. Instead, I used a variety of performance tools and psychological techniques to help him build his self-esteem and self-confidence, and to become aware of his strengths, and then we focused on that. As his confidence grew, his ability to perform in class also grew.

The bottom line is this: While everything we do in performance improvement and performance consulting is valid and valuable, nothing is more important than getting the results people want. When they come to us, they are looking for a way to achieve those results. If we are not confident in our own abilities to guarantee that we can help them generate those results, then we have to get better at what we do. Remember, models and theories don't always get us there. Practical applications of those models and theories that achieve measurable and sustainable results are what really matters.

A Work Example

Performance consultants will like this example because it shows that a training program is not always the answer. I was asked by a hospital administrator to help one department improve their patient (customer) satisfaction ratings. The ratings had been steadily declining for a year, so the training department was called in to administer customer service training to the staff. Everyone was put through a day of smile training, how to make nice to the patient, and some communication skills training. Yet the patient satisfaction ratings did not turn around. Apparently, the "surgery" was a success (high smile ratings for the training), but the patient "died" (no measurable or sustainable change in performance or satisfaction ratings). So I was called in to "stop the bleeding."

The administrator asked me if I could definitely improve the satisfaction ratings. I guaranteed him that I could do so, especially since I had done it in other places before. Plus, I had materials and techniques from several books I had written that would help me.[2] I interviewed the administrator, the department head, several supervisors, and a representative sample of department personnel. During each interview, I checked for knowledge and understanding of customer service skills, meeting or exceeding patient expectations, and resolving patient complaints. Everyone I interviewed knew everything they should be doing skill wise. So what was the problem? Upon further review and inspection, I found out that the relationships among the people in the department were not the best. In fact, there was some animosity between members of the staff, and that translated into patient care. Plus, the patients could pick up on the nonverbal behaviors that communicated the poor relationships among the hospital staff.

I implemented a coaching program that focused solely on building relationships among the staff. We worked on understanding the organizational and individual results of the staff and the patients. We discussed how to communicate better. We set measurable goals and objectives and created performance standards that every staff member could achieve as well as hold the other staff members accountable for achieving.

Within six months, patient satisfaction ratings rose 8 points, from 88 percent to 96 percent. Now you may not think 8 points is a lot, but if you check your own company's satisfaction ratings, you will find how difficult it is to raise them a few points over any period of time, let alone just six months.

What Does Guaranteeing Performance Improvement Do for You?

We can pretty easily describe what guaranteeing performance improvement does for a client: It sets a high level of expectation for them. It allows them to put you on the spot if you make that guarantee. And it enables them to hold you accountable and responsible for the results of your work. Now what does it do for you?

It also makes you accountable and responsible for the results of your work. Yes, it does put you on the spot, but isn't that where you want to be? After all, what better way to achieve higher levels of performance than to guarantee it? That's why when an athlete makes a guarantee that his team will win or that he or she will win, the media makes such a big deal about it. Sports is one area where it is difficult to guarantee the result because there are so many factors beyond the control of the performer. Yet athletes make these guarantees all the time because it actually motivates them to play better. So when you make a guarantee that you can improve performance, you will be more motivated than ever to make it come true. After all, you don't want to be perceived as a liar, or someone who does not deliver on their promises, or someone who has no credibility. You want people and organizations to believe in you, to trust you, and to like you. We all do. So guarantee the performance improvement and then produce. You'll be glad you did.

Effort Management: A Different
Approach to Improving Performance

Everyone wants results. You hear this same mantra all the time, regardless of your field. You can be in training, performance consulting, or human resources. In fact, people tell us that if we get results, senior management will see us as strategic partners. I don't know if the strategic partner idea is true, but I can guarantee you that senior management will better understand your measurable and sustainable results more than they will your programs, processes, and models. Plus, the behaviorists say that results are all that count. If you just positively reinforce the results you want and aversively reinforce the results you don't want, then future behaviors will lead to similar beneficial results. This is true in many cases, but not all. If it was this easy, then everyone would have been guaranteeing performance improvement all along.

As learning and performance professionals, we know about the importance of praise and positive reinforcement. In fact, most people will tell you that praise is good for both the person giving it as well as the person receiving it. When someone tells you how good you are or how well you did something, you always feel better, don't you? Plus, it usually builds your self-esteem to hear good things about yourself from someone else.

Unfortunately, this common wisdom is actually a critical myth. All positive reinforcement does not always lead to more positive results or to improved learning and performance. How many times have you told someone (of any age) something like "You're so smart" or "You did a great job," and then the person refuses to perform again? They get frightened for some reason. Usually it's because they don't think they can achieve the same level of performance, or because they are afraid of what other people will think if they don't achieve that level. Yet because we've all done it, we expect this type of positive reinforcement to motivate the person to do the job or task again and hopefully do it even better the next time.

That brings us to the problem: We are forgetting to provide reinforcement for the effort involved in completing the task. Research in attribution theory (the field of motivational psychology that describes the reasons we give for the results of our performances) tells us conclusively that when we only "reward" or reinforce ability, we run the risk of scaring off the person the next time. Some people are locked in to the fixed mindset or belief that their self-worth is tied up in their innate abilities: being smart, having good looks, being musically inclined, being a natural athlete, having things come easy if you're so good, etc. It's the mistaken philosophy that "I am my job" or "I am whatever I am doing at this moment." When you praise a person's ability or their innate tendencies, you are telling them that they have the power to overcome any obstacles to achieve high performance. This thought, even though it might be true some of the time, might actually frighten performers because now they *have* to succeed the next time. It is expected of them by everyone. When expectations are raised, the pressure mounts, and a fear of success creeps in. And sometimes, fear of success is more debilitating than fear of failure.

On the other hand, when you praise both their effort and their achievement, you will find that people are more willing to do a task again, take on a different or more challenging task, or set their own expectations at a higher level for future performances.[3] People who are told how great they are when they successfully complete an easy task tend to doubt their ability to do as well on a harder task. They want to protect their self-image and self-esteem, so they often choose not to perform the next time around just in case they do not do well. And when they are told how great they are because they did well on a hard task, they have a tendency to back off the next time for fear of not meeting their own or other people's expectations. On the other hand, people who are told specifically about the effort they put in, how they made progress on the way to perfect performance, and how they can continue to learn from what they accomplished are usually more motivated to try again, perform at a higher level, and even request more difficult tasks. There is a great deal of recent research done by Carol Dweck[4] that supports these concepts.

How Praising Results and Ability
Can Hurt Future Effort

Here is an example of what I mean: Take a trip back to a time when your child or a child you know was learning to walk. If you only praised the results or the ability to walk, the child would never get anywhere because a toddler falls more than she stands most of the time. Yet you continue to praise the effort of the child as they rise, stumble a few steps, fall down, and then repeat the process. With each extra step, you are praising both the effort and the improving result. You would never think of telling the toddler how poorly she was walking, or how incompetent she was in learning to perform this task. And it is your constant reinforcement of the effort of the child that leads to the steadily improving performance of walking. So why do we spend so much time only reinforcing results and ability in the workplace when we have examples of how we must combine ability with effort reinforcement?

Another example has to do with youth athletes. Young athletes who are head and shoulders above their peers get constant praise and attention for what they accomplish. Now there can be a variety of reasons for these accomplishments, and they might be valid. However, the problem occurs when the athletes are constantly told how good they are. They are bigger, faster, stronger, smarter, or whatever than other athletes their age. They are so much better that they might even stop putting effort into their athletic performances. Eventually, their performances might decline. If this continues, the young athletes might start to doubt themselves. Then, for some reason, a large majority of them drop out of organized sports in their early teens. The reasons are many, from too much pressure to too many obligations to loss of enjoyment of the sport. There is another reason: the young athlete's perception that he can never or no longer live up to his "publicity." Rather than damage his self-esteem and self-confidence, he drops out of sports altogether. He becomes another casualty of reinforcing results and ability instead of also praising the effort.

So What Do We Do?

I call the concept of how to effectively reinforce this other aspect of learning and performance **effort management**. It requires that everyone help everyone else manage the effort they put into achieving a goal or an objective. Effort varies, and sometimes people put in the proper amount of effort to achieve a goal and sometimes they do not. If they can attribute a result to effort, or lack of effort, they can easily determine what they must do to perform better next time. This is true on both easy and hard tasks, at work and at play, in music and in sports. However, if they attribute what they accomplish to their innate abilities, such as intelligence, strength, good looks, or whatever, and especially if this attribution is for an easy achievement, they will be hard-pressed to try something more difficult next time. That's because they believe they will be evaluated by "observers" who will probably judge them harshly, and they don't want to ruin their image in case they fail. Basically, they have locked themselves in to a fixed mindset about how their innate abilities and not their effort will help them do what they must do, and their entire being becomes wrapped up in the result. People who manage their effort, on the other hand, see every performance and every result as a learning opportunity.

You must build up a person's confidence and self-esteem through reinforcement of the results they achieve related to both their abilities and effort. You must focus on their strengths and help them fully understand what is expected of them regarding the performance results.[5] You cannot just tell them how great they are because then they will possibly lower their expectations and probably their effort for future results in order to save face. Everyone who is in a relationship with the performer (boss, parent, teacher, friend, etc.) must provide positive reinforcement of both effort and ability as it relates to results in order to help the person stay motivated to continue learning and performing at a high level.

When you provide feedback this way, good effort managers use it to improve next time. Failure becomes the fuel to better focus on the next task and do better. Failure becomes feedback that tells performers why they achieved a result that was less than they originally expected. And since their self-confidence remains high, they use the feedback as a motivator to take on a harder task next time and still expect to perform at a high level.

As a trainer, consultant, manager, leader, and/or business owner, you must focus on the effort people put in when they achieve a goal. Tell them about the specifics of what they were doing in order to get to that goal. Don't tell them how smart they were or how much talent they have, unless you have first showed them how their effort led to their result. So manage their effort by specifying the behaviors they displayed to achieve their goals, reinforce the importance of future effort, and then help them understand how effort will always increase ability. Unfortunately, the opposite is not always true; having more ability will not always increase effort. When you employ effort management, you employ top performers and you can guarantee performance improvement.

Now, even with all that said, I am still a firm believer that results matter. I have worked with clients in the past who have taken the "reinforce the effort" approach to heart and have done a great job of positively reinforcing and rewarding the effort of various performers. While this makes for a feel-good situation, a problem occurs when the effort does not lead to desired results, or at least approximations of the desired results. If you are teaching someone to shoot foul shots, and the goal is to make 7 out of 10, and they miss all their foul shots, telling them how well they tried is not going to make them a better foul shooter. Only constant practice will do that. Then, when they are up to 5 or 6 out of 10, you can tell them about the great effort they put in. The same is true in business. Let's say you have a salesperson who is supposed to make 100 phone calls a day. This person makes only 8 calls on a given day. Telling him what a great job he is doing attempting to make phone calls will not get him up to 100 calls for a day. New objectives must be set, and then, over time, this person can increase his call numbers. Reinforcing the successive approximations of the desired objective will be more effective when the performance comes close to accomplishing that objective. Always remember that while effort management is important and sometimes critical, results still matter.

Other Ways to Guarantee Performance Improvement and Get Results that Matter

Why is it that many people in the performance improvement industry—consultants, coaches, trainers—are reluctant to guarantee the results of their interventions? Why are they so afraid of telling their clients or their company that they can definitely create performance improvement? The industry is rock solid when it comes to talking about models, theories, research results, processes, previously effective interventions, flow charts, and cause analysis. So what is the hold up when it comes to telling someone, "Yes, we can guarantee performance improvement"? Are we afraid to go out on a limb, or are we just not sure that we can do it every time.

As I've said before in this book, the motivation and attitudes of the performer play a significant role in any improvement efforts. If the performer does not want to do the task, then the task will not get done, or at least not get done at the highest level. That's why I have said, here and in the past, that you must take into account what the performer is thinking, feeling, and wanting to do in relation to a given performance. Once you've accounted for these factors, you can use any or all of the following techniques to further guarantee performance improvement.

Peak Performance Patterns

Every one of us has experienced a peak performance in some area of our lives. It may have been sports, dancing, playing a musical instrument, painting, reading, making love, being with our children, driving a car, sailing a boat, relaxing on a beach, or any number of other ideas you can come up with. The fact of the matter is that we have all experienced some type of peak performance. The problem is that we don't seem to be able to either sustain that peak performance over time or to have multiple peak performances related to the same task. Here are some things you can do to help you and the people around you experience more peak performances more often.

The first thing to do is select a peak performance that you remember well. Clear and comprehensive memory of the event is crucial to your being able to duplicate the thoughts, feelings, and attitudes in the future. Once you have selected the peak performance event, re-live it in your mind. Go through and over everything you did prior to, during, and after that peak performance. As you go through this in your mind, write down what you were doing. It is as if you are making a step-by-step chart of everything you did. I call this your performance pattern. Each of us has a performance pattern related to a given task or set of tasks. Golfers have their pre-swing ritual, just as basketball players have pre-shot habits before they attempt a foul shot. Baseball players, dancers, musicians—everybody—has a pre-performance ritual that they follow that they feel leads them to a peak performance. The key is for you to identify everything you do before and during your performance so that you can chart it, study it, and repeat it in a similar task situation. Here is a sample of my performance pattern for making a speech:

1. Review notes, handouts, and slides, if they are being used.

2. Visualize the topic headings in my mind.

3. Begin physically stretching as I would before playing basketball.

4. Start walking around to get the blood flowing.

5. Visualize the audience giving me a standing ovation.

6. "Listen" in my mind as the host introduces me.

7. Very quickly see myself giving the speech to a very receptive audience.

8. See the audience giving me a standing ovation again and smiling as they leave the session.

9. Take a few deep breaths.

10. Continue walking around to keep the blood flowing while hearing myself speak.

11. Do some final stretches.

12. Give a great speech that ends with a standing ovation.

Now, it is your turn. Select a peak performance situation from anywhere in your life: business, personal, school, sports. Get a clear memory of it and start to write down the steps you took before, during, and after the peak performance. When you complete the pattern analysis for this task, select another task and see if the same basic pattern applies. If it does, then you have identified what you do to ensure a peak performance. If the patterns differ, you must find similarities in your actions so that you know which behaviors occur in all peak performances.

Performer Name: _____

Performance Name: _____

Steps in Performance Pattern:

1. _____
2. _____
3. _____
4. _____
5. _____
6. _____
7. _____
8. _____
9. _____
10. _____

Remember that there is no set number of steps. You can have either more or fewer steps in your pattern.

Another thing I do with clients is ask them a series of questions about a particular performance to help them identify what they did, determine if the performance met their expectations or the expectations of someone they report to, and see if there is anything they can do to improve on a future but similar performance. Remember: I said previously that results matter. You should always be aware of the results you are trying to achieve, and one of the best ways to increase this awareness is through a self-assessment using some type of questionnaire. Feel free to adapt this job aid to your situation. It is designed so that someone can ask questions of a manager to learn more about a person's performance. Please notice that the wording is in the present tense to enable you to prepare someone for the peak performance. You can just as easily use this after a performance has occurred by changing the verb tense.

Performance Results Analysis Questionnaire

1. What measurable results are you looking to achieve when you perform this task?

2. What are the most desirable results and consequences of performing this task? In other words, what wants and desires of yours are satisfied by a successful performance?

3. What rewards or incentives do you prefer when you successfully complete a task?

4. How do you prefer to be reinforced for performing well: visually, verbally, physically, or financially?

5. If you can't get exactly what you want (reinforcement) for performing well, what would be a satisfactory substitute?

6. What else must be done to offset your disappointment or dissatisfaction if you do not get what you want for performing well?

(Continued)

Performance Results Analysis Questionnaire (concluded)

---

7. What specific conditions must exist for you to perform this task again at a high level?

8. How well did the actual results of the performance match the desired or expected results?

9. What changes must you make in the performance for the next time?

10. What, if anything, would prevent you from performing this task again?

When you get yourself, or a performer you are working with, involved in answering these questions, you are helping assess and analyze the causes, expectations, incentives, and actual behaviors that did lead to, would lead to, or could lead to a peak performance. Modify these questions to better suit your situation. Add other questions if you wish. The important thing is to ask the questions. Many times, performers cannot describe why they did what they did or how they did so well. This brief questionnaire helps a performer recall and structure what occurred relative to a peak performance so that the same things can be done again with the same results. You are then better able to identify and possibly combine the mental, physical, and emotional state of the performer to achieve a peak performance in another situation.

Emotional Control

It is imperative that performers exercise emotional control in order to complete a task at a high level. This does not mean that performers should not have any emotions invested in a performance—quite the contrary. Every performer has some emotional investment each time they do something. There are tasks that are more important, more meaningful, and more personal than other tasks. These tasks will require a high level of emotional investment and, therefore, may also require significant emotional control.

In sport and motivational psychology, we talk about the level of arousal related to a performance. Too much or too little arousal usually leads to a less than stellar performance. Just the right amount of arousal—what some people call optimal arousal or the ideal performance state—more often than not leads to a high level of performance. In the practical world, level of arousal refers to how much anxiety, tension, and pressure a person feels when they are performing. It is fine to be anxious and tense, and feel a certain amount of pressure. The key is to keep those feelings under control. If they are not under control, you will feel too much stress and your performance will deteriorate. Remember the metaphor related to this: It is fine to have butterflies in your stomach before you perform. Just make sure they are flying in the right direction.

In fact, a little bit of tension or anxiety is good for you. It will motivate you to focus better on the task at hand. It will hone your perception of what you have to do and help you eliminate any distractions. The sharper your focus and attention, the greater the chance of doing a good job. Allowing emotions to distract you will negatively affect your performance. Keeping them in check or under control will help you do better. For more information on how to control your emotions, re-read Chapters 3 and 5 in this book. If you're looking for a quick and effective technique to get your emotions under control, here are two:

- The first is deep breathing. Just like when you have to manage your stress, deep breathing relaxes you. It also helps you focus your attention because you start out concentrating just on your breath going in and out. Then you can focus on the task at hand.

- The second technique is positive affirmations. Once you start telling yourself that you are in control of your emotions, you will be. Positive self-talk will give you confidence, increase your self-esteem, and strengthen your belief that you can control your emotions.

Over time, these two techniques will prepare you well for improving performance, achieving at a high level on a consistent basis, and experiencing a peak performance more often than you normally would. Plus, emotional control, either for yourself or people you are working with, will enhance any performer's ability to guarantee performance improvement.

NeuroLinguistic Programming (NLP)

NeuroLinguistic Programming (NLP) is a branch of psychology that focuses on how people represent their perceptions and process information when they are performing. It is how the brain codes experience and helps us understand our subjective experiences, what we call perception. NLP has been used in therapy, academic achievement, sports, peak performance training, sales training, communication skills, and a host of other areas, all with the explicit goal of helping people become better achievers (performers). While describing the entire field of NLP is beyond the scope of this book, here are a few principles and techniques that will help you achieve high levels of performance and virtually guarantee performance improvement in most situations.

Let's start with your belief systems. Everyone has different levels of beliefs, but we all have either enabling or disabling beliefs. Enabling beliefs help us perform better while disabling beliefs cause us to fail. These beliefs can manifest themselves as images we hold in our minds, things we say to ourselves, or voices we replay in our minds from what other people tell us. If you think back to the earlier section on effort management in this chapter, you will realize that reinforcing effort can have a positive or a negative effect on a person and future performances, depending on how close the result of the current effort was to the desired result. Improper effort reinforcement can lead to improper belief systems, while proper reinforcement can lead to appropriate belief systems.

Look at the table below. It lists several areas of your life where you can have either enabling or disabling (or self-limiting) beliefs. For this exercise, write down in the proper column your beliefs in each category. Obviously, you want to have more enabling beliefs than disabling beliefs. The key to high performance and getting results that you want is your ability to reduce or remove the disabling beliefs from your mind (system). It is up to you to choose if your belief system will hold you back or move you forward.

Self-Limiting and Enabling Beliefs

In the columns below, fill in your self-limiting and enabling beliefs for the 10 areas of life listed. Be as specific and descriptive as possible. When you finish this exercise, you should have a comprehensive list of what holds you back from achieving your goals in each area of your life and what you have to do to move forward.

Life Area	Self-Limiting Beliefs	Enabling Beliefs
Mental		
Physical		
Personal		
Professional		
Family		
Community		
Financial		
Social		
Knowledge		
Society		

The following NLP patterns are applicable to any peak performance situation. Peak performers often find themselves using one or more of these patterns, even though they may be unaware of what they are actually doing. An understanding of these NLP patterns will help anyone replicate them and achieve a peak performance state in any situation.

NLP Patterns for Improved and Peak Performance

1. **Resourceful self.** The peak performer is capable of recreating, from the past, a peak performance that contained all the resources required to do the same thing again in the current situation. The resourceful self pattern helps the peak performer experience all the sights, sounds, and feelings of the past peak performance and then bring those experiences into the present. It gives the performer confidence and inner strength.

2. **Changing beliefs.** Peak performers must always maintain a positive mental attitude and a high level of motivation. Both of these states are based on an internal belief system. The ability to change beliefs from negative to positive and to strengthen already existing positive beliefs helps peak performers maintain their edge. Refer back to the table you just completed on disabling and enabling beliefs and develop an action plan to remove or revise any disabling beliefs.

3. **New behavior generator.** Peak performers always try to find an excellent role model before attempting any new behavior. When they can't find someone, and they themselves do not possess the set of skills necessary to exhibit a peak performance in a given situation, they actually go out and create (manufacture) the desired new behaviors they require in order to produce a superior performance. Since one of the principles of NLP is that we already have the resources we require inside of us or available to us, we use that principle to generate new behaviors that will lead to performance improvement.

4. **Timeline/Changing past histories.** Anyone can achieve a peak performance, even if they have never done so before. People can access their personal timeline, such as their past, present, and/or future (desired) behaviors. Then they can go back in their minds to change any past behaviors to make themselves more resourceful, powerful, and successful. Peak performers are then able to bring these past, resourceful behaviors forward to the present and future along the timeline and continue to exhibit and possess the resourceful behaviors whenever they are required. Even if they were unsuccessful in the past, this NLP technique helps performers rid themselves of that earlier result and prepare themselves for improved performance in the future.

5. **Reframing.** Performances are sometimes stopped by what appears to be a negative behavior. In reality, every behavior has a positive intention (another NLP principle). We might not know exactly what that positive intention is just yet. Reframing helps the peak performer understand the positive intention of the apparently limiting behavior and then use that positive intention to foster peak performances in other situations. Reframing also helps a person alter their negative perceptions of a task, situation, or previous result so that they are capable of improving future performances.

6. **Visual-kinesthetic dissociation.** Sometimes people are limited in their capability to achieve by an unknown fear. This approach to dissociation enables the peak performer to identify and overcome the limiting fear or belief, create appropriate new and positive behaviors, and then use them to achieve peak performance. They do this by first visualizing themselves in a new and positive situation, then feeling themselves perform in that situation, and finally taking the new behaviors they just experienced and transferring them to the current situation.

7. **Swish.** This mental rehearsal approach simply switches a non-supporting behavior with a supporting behavior or a positive behavior with a negative one. Using a variety of imagery and submodality techniques (submodalities are the qualities and characteristics that make an image or a behavior compelling or important to us and also refer to how we code the information in our brains), the peak performer can actually "swish" or "switch" the two behaviors. Then the positive behavior becomes the one that is activated in appropriate situations.

8. **Kinesthetic access pattern.** Peak performers are always in touch with their bodies, sensations, and feelings. This pattern enables them to access those same sensations plus the associated submodalities from previous peak performances. Then the kinesthetic sensations, motor programs, and submodalities can be redesigned or transferred as they are required for future peak performances. Basically, you are able to constantly draw on past positive experiences to get a feel for the current performance situation.

9. **Outcome frame.** This is one of the easiest NLP techniques to overlook, especially when trying to achieve peak performance. Peak performers are well aware of what they are trying to achieve. They know exactly what their preferred, positive perk performance result is. They know when they want to achieve it, what the evidence will be that tells them they have achieved it, and what the criteria are that determines they have successfully completed the peak performance. They are also aware of the positive impact the successful completion of this performance will have on their lives. This technique fits in with my philosophy that results matter and what has been talked about related to SMARTER objectives. When you begin with the end in mind, you will do everything possible to achieve that positive end (result and accomplishment).

10. **Anchoring.** Anchoring is establishing a trigger relationship between a stimulus and a desired response. Peak performers know how to fully experience a previous peak performance. They see the sights, hear the sounds, and feel the feelings of that earlier achievement. Then, when they are fully into re-living the experience, they create an anchor (a trigger) that will associate that experience to the present. Then, whenever they are in a similar situation, they trigger the positive response and bring all the skills, capabilities, feelings, and experiences of the past into the present situation. This is known as "firing off the anchor." For example, let's say you visualize a previous peak performance. You get into the "zone" of that experience and are feeling all the good things you felt while it was actually happening. Now you touch your left index finger to your right elbow. This becomes your anchor trigger, so any time you want to fire off this anchor, you touch your left index finger to your right elbow. With enough practice, the anchor will fire off automatically and you can't help but experience a higher level of performance than what would have been expected.

These 10 NLP skills have been shown to be the most closely associated with peak performance. These skills can be taught to anyone, who can then use them to achieve a peak performance in any given situation. Or a "coach" can help a person achieve peak performance by using these NLP skills. The 10 NLP skills, when used throughout the peak performance process, have led to peak performances in athletics, public speaking, group dynamics, individual and group decision making, education, learning, sales, law, and personal relationships. And since all these techniques focus on the performer directly, it is very easy to see how using any or all of these techniques will guarantee performance improvement in most, if not all, situations.

Mental Rehearsal

The concept of mental rehearsal seems to naturally follow emotion control and NLP. Mental rehearsal is simply playing the performance over and over again in your mind before you actually go out and do it. A variety of mental rehearsal techniques exist. The ones we are most familiar with are imagery and visualization. While most people think they are the same, there is a slight difference. Imagery involves getting static pictures of what you want to do in your mind, while visualization requires you to take those static pictures and put them "into play." In other words, visualization involves making a mental movie to rehearse your tasks.

How well does mental rehearsal work? Just ask any top athlete, professional speaker, dancer, or any other type of high-level performer. They will all tell you that they use mental rehearsal. The reasons vary, but here are some of them:

- Mental rehearsal is actually quicker than physical practice. You can play a 4-hour round of golf in your mind in 30 minutes.

- Mental rehearsal does activate the neuromuscular system that you would use if you were physically performing a task. That's because the mind really does not know the difference between a real or an imagined event.

- Mental rehearsal improves your performance levels in all situations above no practice at all, and in some situations, it improves performance as well as physical practice does.

- When you combine mental rehearsal with physical practice, you are guaranteed to get a higher level of performance than with either approach alone.

So if mental rehearsal works so well, why don't we spend more time using it? The answer is, I don't know. I've used it personally all my life and I teach my coaching clients to use the technique. Positive results that occur in people's minds make them feel better about themselves and feel more confident. As their confidence increases, they are more motivated to take on challenging tasks. Their enabling belief system grows, and they truly believe they will achieve their performance objectives. If system interventions and organizational interventions, for example, don't work, performers should mentally rehearse the best ways to get a job done. They will most likely find a way to overcome any obstacles and achieve improved performance, first in their minds and then when they actually perform.

One other note about mental rehearsal is important: It is one of the main techniques used in stress management. When people are under stress, they are taught first to breathe slowly and deeply, then to visualize themselves in a calm and relaxing place. Once they are "on the beach or floating on a cloud," they are taught to rehearse the coping responses (positive behaviors) that will help them reduce their stress, overcome their obstacles, and achieve their objectives. Mental rehearsal is a powerful technique for performance improvement. It is used a great deal by athletes, and it should be used more often than it is in other situations. People, organizations, and societies would all be "better" if performers spent time mentally rehearsing their actions and results before jumping into a performance.

Motivation Maximization

This is not so much a technique as a category heading. It is critical that we are able to maximize a performer's motivation as it relates to a specific performance and desired result. For example, let's say you have taught someone to drive a race car. You have checked out the car, and it is in perfect condition. The performer has learned how to drive it on previous occasions. You offer the keys to the performer. At this point, everything is ready. The system (car and track) are prepared perfectly. The driver has been trained (the intervention has been implemented). The entire system is a go. So you offer the keys, and the driver says, "Nope, not today. I just don't feel like it."

What happened? Everything was done as it was supposed to be done. Yet the driver (performer) refused to drive because he didn't feel like it. What was missing? You already know the answer. The driver was not motivated to drive on this occasion. How many situations have you been in where everything should have occurred perfectly, yet didn't? People have the skills to achieve, they have been trained to do the job, and they are capable of achieving their objectives. But the reason they don't achieve is usually because the performer is not motivated or lacks motivation to perform.

The solution to the motivation problem is to find out how to maximize the preferred motivation of the performer. Most people are either approachers or avoiders. They will either move toward a goal (approach) or away from it (avoid). The problem here is that avoidance motivation is more powerful than approach motivation. For example, most people would prefer to move away from pain than to approach pleasure. That is because pain is so distasteful and disheartening, and it can hurt (physically and emotionally). So people move away from that instead of seek out pleasure. One way to guarantee a motivated performer is to find out if she is an approach person or an avoidance person, and then structure the situation accordingly.

Other areas of motivation that we have to look at include the performer's desire to achieve, their requirement for affiliation (making friends and being liked), and their desire for power (being in charge or in control). All these factors play into what will motivate someone to perform a task. You also must consider how well they expect to perform, what they believe will happen to them when they are finished performing, the types of rewards and reinforcements they prefer, and how they will respond if someone provides them with feedback on their performance. All these factors come into play when a person decides if she is motivated enough to effectively and successfully complete a task.

Use the following job aid to rate your motivation for a given task. The first time, pick a task that you like. Then select a task you dislike. Rate your motivation for each and identify the differences. Now, ask yourself about the causes of these differences and how your differing motivation levels affect the results of the performances.

Rating My Motivation

Think about a task that you like to perform and also one that you dislike. Then, in the appropriate columns, rate your level of motivation in each area using a scale of 0 to 10, where 0 means no motivation of that type and 10 means extremely high motivation of that type. Then compare the differences in your ratings.

Motivation	Task I Like	Task I Dislike
Achievement		
Affiliation		
Power		
Approach		
Avoidance		

It seems intuitively obvious that by focusing on a performer's motivation, you can help them achieve their objectives, improve their performances in given situations, and develop high levels of self-confidence so that they will undertake challenging tasks in the future because they expect to do well. Get enough people in an organization thinking and performing like this and you'll be pleasantly surprised at what everyone accomplishes as individuals and what the organization accomplishes as an entity.

One more thing about maximizing motivation, and I make no apologies to the performance technology purists for these comments. While the purists focus on systems, interventions, and technologies or theories supported by research (and I do believe that this is important), I invite them to also look inside the performer. I have never met a person who did not want to be appreciated for who they are and what they've accomplished. I've also never met someone who did not like positive reinforcement, personalized rewards, and a little recognition for their achievements. And finally, I've never met a person who did not want to be respected. In fact, I would venture to say that if you show and tell someone you appreciate them for who they are and what they are doing, recognize their accomplishments in a positive manner, and respect them as an individual, I'll bet that you will get them to run through brick walls for you, go to the ends of the earth for you, and climb the highest mountain for you. They will do all this just so that they can hear it and feel it from you all over again.

Does it work? I can give you countless anecdotes from my consulting and coaching career on how these simple motivational approaches have helped people achieve stellar performances. By using a positive approach when I coached youth basketball, my teams won several league championships even though we clearly did not have the best talent. By asking people what they wanted in terms of rewards and reinforcements, I helped a client company increase sales by 27 percent in one year. By respecting at-risk students for what they already knew, I was able to help them achieve at grade level and get promoted to the next grade instead of being kept back. And I can go on and on, as I'm sure you can.

The bottom line is that if you want to guarantee performance improvement and positively affect your bottom line, learn how to maximize the motivation of your performers. Take a look at the following 20 hidden motivators that you can draw on to help maximize motivation and improve performance. Then study 20 other ways you can motivate people on the job to do a better job. You will be pleasantly surprised at the results you and your people will achieve when you maximize motivation.

20 Hidden Motivators

Power	Socialization/Friendship/Family
Fear/Threat	Status
Desire	Recognition/Appreciation
Anger/Hate/Revenge	Self-improvement
Honor/Integrity	Sympathy
Confidence	Altruism (greater good)
Creativity	Sincerity
Love	Touch
Food	Safety/Security
Money	Knowledge/Learning

20 Ways to Motivate Employees

Make work interesting	Provide training
Make work fun	Improve the work environment
Offer flextime	Speak positively
Rotate jobs	Be a role model
Enrich jobs	Individualize rewards
Increase customer contact	Reinforce job impact
Set realistic goals	Increase job satisfaction
Set high expectations	Celebrate small and large wins
Challenge employees	Provide opportunities for individual and professional growth
Respect employees	
Provide feedback	

Endnotes

1. See Gerson, R. F., & Gerson, R. G., (2006). *Positive performance improvement: A new paradigm for optimizing your workforce.* Palo Alto, CA: Davies-Black.

2. Gerson, R. F., (1998). *Beyond customer service.* Menlo Park, CA: Crisp Publications; Gerson, R. F., (1993). *Measuring customer satisfaction.* Menlo Park, California. Crisp Publications.

3. This has been shown to be true using expectancy theory and attribution theory. Additionally, when you reward effort that leads to a successful result or closely approximates a successful result, you will motivate performers to attempt more challenging tasks.

4. Dweck, C., (2006). *Mindset: The new psychology of success.* New York: Random House.

5. See Note 1. Also Gerson, R. F., (2004). *HEADcoaching: Mental training for peak performance.* Bloomington, IN: Authorhouse.

Chapter 7
Models for Success

Results matter. We've already established that fact at the beginning of the book and throughout its pages. Now it's time to provide you with some specific roadmaps to help you guarantee performance improvement. These models of success have been proven and tested to be effective in a variety of settings. The models presented here are by no means all the models you can use to be successful when you perform, nor are they meant to be the final word on what you should do, use, or produce to help someone else improve their performance. The models are simply guides to help you get from where you are now to where you want to be.

Remember that a model is a visual representation of a process. Throughout this book, I have urged you not to get bogged down in processes to the exclusion of your desired results. These models provide processes you can follow on your way to achieving your desired results. Stay focused on your ultimate achievement, not so much on how to get there. Let the models be your guide, but don't let them blind you to the importance of beginning with the end in mind, accomplishing your tasks, and getting measurable and sustainable results from all your performances.

The Organizational Elements Model (OEM)

Kaufman has written about the OEM in more publications than you would care to imagine. His premise is simple: Different levels of performance require different thinking and doing. For example, the objectives of an individual differ from those of an organization, which differ from those of society as a whole. The OEM puts these things in perspective so that you can determine which level you are working at and whether or not you are close to achieving the Ideal Vision, which Kaufman calls Mega.[1] Here is what the model looks like in chart form:

Kaufman's Organizational Elements Model

Name of the Organizational Element	Brief Description and Level of Focus	Type of Thinking and Planning
Mega (society)	Results and their consequences for external clients and society (shared vision)	Strategic
Macro (organization)	The results and their consequences for what an organization can or does deliver outside of itself	Tactical
Micro (individual)	The results and their consequences for individuals and small groups within the organization	Operational
Process	Means, programs, projects, activities, methods, techniques	
Input	Human, capital, and physical resources; existing rules, regulations, policies, laws	

The premise behind the OEM is for everyone to think about what they do, use, and produce and how it benefits the "ultimate client," society. The objective is to make a measurable contribution that makes the world a better place. This concept translates very well into individual performance and the approach taken in this book that you can actually guarantee performance improvement. Here is an adaptation of the OEM for helping people and organizations go from good to great to better than great. It uses the concept of an individual who is trying to lose weight. Now most people who attempt to lose weight only focus on the short-term gain of dropping a few pounds. By putting this process into an OEM format, you can easily see how much more motivating the concept of weight loss becomes.

Achieving the Ideal Vision for an Individual

Input What I'd like to do	Process How I'd like to do it	Micro My short-term goal	Macro My audacious goal	Mega My ultimate goal
Lose weight	Dieting	Lose 10 pounds	Be fit and have energy	Live a long, healthy life free from illness

The same is true for an organization. Once companies get it into their "heads" that whatever they do must benefit society and that this "lofty objective" will actually be much more motivating to employees, then you will not have to guarantee performance improvements ever again. They will be happening constantly.

Achieving the Ideal Vision for an Organization

Input What I'd like to do	Process How I'd like to do it	Micro My short-term goal	Macro My audacious goal	Mega My ultimate goal
Retain employees	Human capital management	Reduce turnover by 5%	Keep all high performing employees 10+ years	Make a strong, positive contribution to society by preserving institutional memory

The OEM makes a strong case for the concept of begin with the end in mind. If every performer and organization within which that performer operates began with the positive benefits of the performance for society, then the performer or performers would naturally become intrinsically motivated to get better, do a better job, and make the world a better place to live. This concept seems so logical that it makes you wonder why everyone does not approach their performance situations in this manner. The concept of Mega should be a guiding light for all performers as they strive to achieve perfect performance.[2]

Performance Assessment Matrix

Here is a simple model that I use when I coach individual performers. It helps you focus on their competencies, behaviors, and accomplishments—all the components of performance. The rating scale gives you a "measure" of what they have achieved to date and what has to be done to get them to the next level. Once performers know what is expected of them, and the desired objectives and results are made clear to them, their performance naturally improves.

The best way to use this matrix is to work with an individual performer and assess her competencies first. Does she possess the knowledge, skills, and abilities to do the job? Once you determine this, you must decide on what percentage of the required competencies she actually does possess. Then you rate her accordingly. In this example, a rating of 1 is the best. You can reverse the ratings if you are more comfortable (your mental model) having a higher rating signify a better score. Next, you rate the appropriateness of the behaviors related to the performance. Use the same rating scale to "score" the behaviors. Finally, determine if she has achieved all or a specific percentage of the originally agreed-upon performance objectives.

Once you have completed the matrix, share the "scorecard" with the performer. Her natural curiosity and desire to do better will motivate her to improve in any area where she did not receive a top score. It will be up to you to provide some methods and means for her to improve her performance, but at least you will know what areas she must work in. This simple scoreboard approach very often has a powerful effect on a performer. They actually become self-motivated to do better, and that alone can guarantee performance improvement.

Performance Assessment Matrix

Category/Ranking	1	2	3
Accomplishments			
Behaviors			
Competencies			

Accomplishments: Did the performer achieve his or her objectives (5–10 minimum)

    90 percent achievement of all objectives = 1
    80 percent achievement of all objectives = 2
    70 percent achievement of all objectives = 3

Behaviors: Does the performer exhibit appropriate performance behaviors?

    90 percent of appropriate behaviors identified = 1
    80 percent of appropriate behaviors identified = 2
    70 percent of appropriate behaviors identified = 3

Competencies: Does the performer possess the competencies required to effectively complete the job?

    90 percent of required competencies possessed = 1
    80 percent of required competencies possessed = 2
    70 percent of required competencies possessed = 3

Speaking of scorecards, here is another job aid that I use to coach my individual and team clients to higher levels of performance. It is simply called the Performance Analysis SCORE Card, and the completion of it is really self-explanatory. You just fill in the boxes with the appropriate information in text form, and then assign a numerical value (I use a scale of 1 to 10 with 10 being the best/highest score possible) to each of the first three boxes. This gives you a visual of how close or how far you are from achieving your desired objectives. It also lets you know which area of the scorecard requires the most attention and work. Plus, the assignment of numerical values allows you to plot a graph of the scorecard for a pictorial representation. You cannot initially assign a numerical value to the last two boxes because they have not occurred yet. Below is a sample completed scorecard. You can use this in as many situations as you require.

Performance Analysis SCORE Card

Situation	Causes	Options	Results	Evaluation
What Is vs. What Should Be (current/ desired)	Resources: Organizational/ Individual	Interventions/ Solutions/ Opportunities	Goal Statement: Qualitative/ Quantitative	Measurements/ Feedback and Impact
Sales are at 70% of plan instead of 90 to 100% (7 rating)	Too few appointments, not enough proposals (5)	Review of lead generation system, CRM, possible training programs (7)	Achieve 90% of plan within 6 months through increased appointments	Number of: • Appointments • Proposals • New sales • Repurchases • Returns or refunds

This job aid is another form of a scorecard. Remember that when people see their performances translated into numbers, graphs, or word pictures, they are more likely to want to do better the next time. That is why many organizations place performance charts in visible and conspicuous places for employees to see. When people see their own scores, and then see them in comparison to the achievements of others, they usually motivate themselves to do better the next time. This is true also for top performers, who may have nothing to improve, but simply want to enhance their strengths so that they can achieve even higher levels of performance.

Positive CORE: A New Approach
to Performance Improvement

Another model that is very useful is called Positive CORE.[3]
Here is an analogy: Anyone who exercises regularly or works
out with a personal trainer knows that a major focus of high-
level fitness is to have a strong core. Your core is defined as
your abdominal, hip, and back muscles, which basically support
your entire body. That's why there is such an intense focus on
strengthening the core for people who want to attain overall fitness.

The focus on building a strong CORE began over 20 years
ago, except that it was to develop more "fit" business professionals. The objective then, as it still is now, was to link performance interventions and performance improvement to an
enhancement process. I started focusing on strengths back
then and I continue to focus on them throughout this book.
While I called the programs Performance Enhancement Programs at that time, instead of Positive CORE, they were definitely the precursor to this new approach to performance
enhancement.

Positive CORE is an approach to performance improve-
ment/enhancement that was designed based on sport psychology, positive psychology, and appreciative inquiry. With this
approach, performance consultants can identify the CORE
elements of an individual performer that make him successful.
While you can get a great deal of information from observing
one single performer and interviewing him about his performances, you can also involve all the stakeholders of an organization in an effort to determine, define, and describe how the
performance contributions of each individual have led the
organization to where it is, why, and how it functions as it does,
and how it accomplishes what it does. Positive CORE then
seeks to take the organization to another level of performance
by making it more effective, productive, and successful in all
areas by upgrading the current mental make-up, strengths, and
motivational involvement of its individual performers.

The primary focus of Positive CORE is to identify successes and strengths rather than weaknesses and areas for improvements. Now this may seem a little counter-intuitive considering the book is titled Guaranteeing Performance Improvement; however, there is no discrepancy here. The emphasis is placed on strengths to create a "multiplier effect" so that they are increased and leveraged. A focus on strengths will always motivate a performer to do better, which results in a measurable and sustainable performance improvement (in whatever manner you choose to define the term). The focus on the positive puts people in a better frame of mind, motivates them more to continue to achieve, and creates a virtuous cycle of success seeking success.

The elements of the Positive CORE program for individual performers are **C**onfidence, **O**utcomes, **R**elationships, and **E**ngagement. Each of these elements has sub-categories that make it up and are identified in the Positive CORE Elements chart.

Positive CORE Elements

Confidence	Outcomes	Relationships	Engagement
Self-esteem	Objectives, expectations, and reinforcements based on adding value to external clients	Managers	Commitment
Strengths and talents	Measurement and evaluation and continual improvement	Friends and family	Emotions
Reinforcements and consequences	Results and returns: financial, personal, and society	Social, professional, and community	Motivation and optimism

The elements of the Positive CORE model are self-explanatory. If you want to build a person's confidence, help them build their self-esteem, play to their strengths and talents, and make sure the reinforcements and consequences fit the performance results. To make the desired results clear to the performer, let her know the exact expectations related to the performance, how the performance results will be measured and evaluated, and how the results affect her, her organization, her community, and her society. Also, emphasize the importance of the relationships the person is involved in, starting with how she perceives herself, and her relationships with her boss, family, friends, and colleagues. Our social support network goes a long way to determining how "high we fly" when we perform. Finally, make sure the performer is committed to achieving the objectives, is intrinsically motivated, and is bringing her full attention to the task at hand.

When you follow this model, you will get the results you are looking for. The Positive CORE program results in performance improvement and performance enhancement because there is buy-in from the performers (they are totally engaged), the focus on strengths and previous successes creates an ongoing positive atmosphere in which performance takes place, and the organization finds it easier to implement the "new" performance culture because its people are more motivated. Following are two examples of Positive CORE.[4]

Positive CORE and Sales Success: A Practical Example

Implementation of Positive CORE is very easy to accomplish, especially in a sales environment. We all know that sales success is easily measured, sales strengths are easily identified, and the psychobehavioral and motivational make-up of salespeople virtually energizes them to constantly improve.

One organization with 175 salespeople found itself to be stagnant relative to its sales growth. The individual reps were doing as well as in previous years, but no one was growing their share of the business. As such, the company began handing out negative consequences when reps did not meet daily objectives and quarterly quotas. Still, performance did not improve, so the company put everyone through a standard sales training program. Again, there was no measurable increase in performance. Obviously, what they were doing was not achieving their desired results.

We began the Positive CORE process with the sales managers. After going through the four categories and their sub-categories (see the chart above), a clearer picture emerged of the desired culture versus the current culture of the organization, the strengths of its performers, when they were at their best, who had the strongest relationships, who knew what was expected of them, how they became engaged in a task, and how the company and the individuals defined sales excellence. This "profile" was then described and "taught" to the rest of the sales force.

The initial results were encouraging as more sales reps started hitting their numbers. The Positive CORE approach was expanded to include work in the area of intrinsic motivation and development of higher levels of self-confidence. This was then followed by a unique sales training program that taught all the reps the principles of psychobehavioral selling, influential communication (for both inside and outside the company), and the art of asking questions and listening. These skills enhanced the existing strengths of the sales force while simultaneously improving the CORE elements.

The result of the entire Positive CORE intervention was an increase in sales (the measurement program is still ongoing), an increase in the confidence of the sales reps as they engaged in more client-centered behaviors, and a change in the corporate culture from internally competitive to cooperative.

Positive CORE and Performance Enhancement: A Practical Management Example

A large healthcare organization was having difficulty achieving high performance with one of its departments. Each of the department managers was well-trained and dedicated to the organization. Yet the department as a whole only met their base objectives or performed slightly below their baselines. This did not seem to make sense, so we were asked to determine how to turn this group into high performers.

Positive CORE interviews were conducted, which determined that, while each of the managers possessed the competencies to perform well, their performance objectives and expectations were not clearly spelled out. They were sort of operating in the dark without a scorecard because they did not have quantifiable measurements (results) to shoot for. Plus, the department head was the strong, silent type, until something went wrong. Then he became very vocal and easily pointed out the mistakes his people were making. This prevented the managers from being totally engaged in their performances.

The interviews also uncovered the strengths of each of the managers. It was suggested to them that they enumerate their strengths to the department head, develop their own performance objectives and results measurements, and then present these to the department head. Since the managers now owned the performance activities, their intrinsic motivation to perform and achieve should increase. And it did. We convinced the department head to let his managers run with the ball based on what they created. His agreement helped the managers become even more engaged in their attempts to enhance current performance levels and improve whatever had to be improved.

The results were excellent. In three months, the entire department had exceeded previous performance metrics and was consistently outperforming their colleagues. The managers had taken ownership of their performance requirements and were totally responsible and accountable for their own consequences. This led to constant engagement on their parts, and each manager became a cheerleader for other managers. We also coached the department head to praise his people when appropriate and take a step back and not jump on them when he saw them doing something wrong. Most people know when they have made a mistake, and pointing it out to them is not always necessary. Plus, when all you do is point out mistakes without ever giving praise or positive reinforcement, you will eventually lose your effectiveness.

The results of this Positive CORE approach led to increased performances across the entire management team—a trickle down effect where employees also increased perform-ance—and a change in leadership behavior for the department head. One year following this approach, the department was the most profitable in the healthcare organization, the depart-ment head was promoted to senior vice president, and several of the managers became department heads. All in all, not bad results for everyone involved.

Why Positive CORE Works (and Worked)

The reason Positive CORE works as an approach to perform-ance improvement is because it focuses on the positive aspects of performance. You tell the performer where they are already good or great and work with them to make them even better. This motivates them to continue performing and improving (remember how you used positive reinforcement to help your child learn to walk?). Now, a virtuous cycle is created within the organization where everyone is intent on getting better plus helping their colleagues improve their perform-ances.

Another Way to Use Positive CORE

Now that you are familiar with the Positive CORE model, here is an easy-to-use checklist that will help you determine which aspects of the model are working for you now and which areas you have to concentrate on in order to improve. The instruc-tions in the checklist ask you to check off those statements that are applicable to you, then identify the items that are not checked. The non-checked items indicate areas for potential improvement. You can also place a numerical value next to each item, using a scale of 1 to 5 or 1 to 10, whichever you prefer. This numerical value provides you with a scorecard measure that identifies the level of effectiveness or achieve-ment within each area of the Positive CORE model. You can use the individual line item ratings as your guide, total up the ratings for each sub-category and category, or create an index score by adding up your ratings and dividing by 12 (the total number of sub-categories). Any way you choose to do it, you will give yourself a representation of how well you are doing by using this model.

Positive CORE Checklist for Individuals

Place a checkmark next to each statement that is true for you. The checkmarks will indicate your core areas of strength, which you must work on to make even stronger. Those items that are not checked indicate areas for improvement. Every two statements correspond to a sub-category in the Positive CORE chart.

☐ I believe in my ability to accomplish things.

☐ I am responsible for my own performance results.

☐ I am aware of my three greatest strengths as a performer.

☐ My organization helps me "play to my strengths."

☐ My organization appreciates its people.

☐ My organization promotes rewards and consequences for performance.

☐ I have written down my goals and objectives.

☐ I know what is expected of me by my organization.

☐ We measure all our performance results.

☐ Our performance measurement system is fully understood by everyone.

☐ I know the financial return on investment (ROI) that my performance achieves for my company.

☐ My organization uses my ROI contribution to determine how much more it invests in me.

☐ I evaluate my performance results in line with my objectives.

☐ My organization measures my performance both qualitatively and quantitatively.

☐ I have developed action plans to achieve my goals.

(continued)

Positive CORE Checklist for Individuals (concluded)

❏   Our people step up to help others achieve their results.
❏   I understand how my performance results affect people, my organization, and society.
❏   I apply my strengths to the betterment of other people, my organization, and society.
❏   I am committed to being highly successful.
❏   My company has identified our top performers and how they do what they do.
❏   I am aware of how my emotions affect my performance.
❏   My organization stresses the importance of emotional intelligence, control, and resiliency.
❏   I am more intrinsically motivated to perform well than extrinsically motivated.
❏   I use an appropriate blend of optimism and activation to achieve and exceed my goals.

Maximizing Motivation and Guaranteeing Performance Improvement

How would you like to learn about a way to virtually guarantee you will get the job done and achieve higher levels of performance? This "tool" will help you identify motivational and performance factors that contribute to high performance as well as any roadblocks that may be holding you, or someone you work with, back. It is called the **Talent Optimization Performance System (TOPS),** and it is a tool I developed through my work coaching and training athletes, executives, and salespeople.[5] Basically, it is a guide to talent optimization, motivational engagement, and guaranteed performance improvement. It identifies 10 areas of performance-related factors (such as motivation, individual beliefs, organizational culture, and stress) that may be the source of performance strengths or the cause of performance problems. The areas are:

Competence (skills and abilities)

Confidence (belief in oneself and one's ability to achieve performance objectives)

Consequence (reinforcers for performance, both positive and negative)

Commitment (dedication to successfully completing a task)

I call this first set the big four of motivation and performance improvement. They are followed by the supporting six:

Communication (how clearly performance expectations are communicated)

Challenge (how challenging the task is)

Conflict (how much stress or conflict exists for the performer)

Culture (how well the organization promotes and rewards successful performances)

Control (how much performers believe they control the consequences)

Concentration (how much attention performers pay to the task and for how long)

When a person's performance continues at a high level, as with most top performers, you can be relatively certain that many or all of these factors are in play. When a person's performance deteriorates, or has never been up to par, you can usually be sure that if it is motivation related, it is due to something that is lacking in one of the above categories. It is up to managers and companies to identify the cause of the performance problem using this TOPS model and then develop potential resolutions for the problems.

For example, if competence is the issue, then more skill training may be necessary, job aids may be required, or a job change may be in order. If the performer lacks confidence, then a series of performance activities that are similar to the required performance must be developed where this person can be successful so that he builds up his confidence and self-esteem. When success is achieved, the positive behaviors and consequences that occurred must be reinforced with praise so that the person will continue to perform well.

When performance standards or expectations are not clearly communicated, then the performer has no idea what constitutes a successful result. Or if the person is under so much stress that she is unable to perform, we must find ways to minimize that stress and maximize a positive performance environment. And if something is distracting her from focusing on the performance, we must teach her how to maintain her attention and concentration so that the task can be completed at a high level.

Solutions to Motivation-related Performance Problems

The most effective solution to any problem is to ask the employee first what is going on. Too often, managers identify a problem and they are the ones who prescribe the answers. They tell the employee what to do, how to do it, and when it must be done. Then the managers wonder why it either never gets done or it does not reach the specified performance level. The reason is simple: The manager owns the solution while the employee still owns the apparent problem. At no time was the employee/performer involved in generating the solution. It may be that the employee never even acknowledged that a problem existed in the first place. This presents an even greater barrier to performance improvement because the performer is unaware or refuses to become aware of a performance deficit.

So to identify and solve any motivation and performance problems, ask your employees first what they perceive the issues and solutions to be. Then go down the list of the 10

areas related to motivation, engagement, and high performance to help them identify other causes. And finally, work with
them to implement the appropriate performance improvement
intervention. This approach will resolve 80 to 90 percent of your
employee motivation and performance improvement problems,
regardless of your industry.

The Talent Optimization Performance System (TOPS)

For a more comprehensive review of the interview process that
can accompany the use of the TOPS, see some of my previous
works.[6] The rating scale presented below is quite sufficient to
help you identify factors that relate to performance strengths as
well as weaknesses. If you are coaching a performer, you may
want to have the performer fill out the rating scale at the same
time you complete it for him or her. It will be interesting to see if
there are different perceptions between the two of you regarding how well he or she performs and what affects his or her
performance.

The graphic representation allows both the manager and
the performer to identify areas that require improvement as well
as areas of greatest strength. Nine of the TOPS factors have
scales moving in a positive direction (10 = strength), with Conflict showing lower numbers to indicate that managing stress
and conflict is a strength. If a factor is rated 7 or less, or if Conflict is rated 3 or higher, then some sort of intervention is
required. A simple change in one or several of these areas
could lead to measurable and sustainable performance
improvements. With this chart, you are taking the "messy middle" (the part we can't see externally) of a performer's motivation and emotional involvement with a performance and making
it visible. Plus, a retest in 30, 60, or 90 days can show a
change in the profile that would correlate to a change in
performance, either positive or negative.

TOPS Rating Scales

Circle the number that best represents your response to the question associated with the TOPS factor.

COMPETENCE: Do I have the skills to do this job?

0	1	2	3	4	5	6	7	8	9	10

I do not possess the skills.

I possess some of the skills.

I possess all of the skills.

CONFIDENCE: How much do I believe I can do this job well?

0	1	2	3	4	5	6	7	8	9	10

I cannot perform this job as expected.

I may be able to perform this job satisfactorily.

I will successfully perform this job.

CONSEQUENCE: Will the consequence (reinforcements) be tied to my results?

0	1	2	3	4	5	6	7	8	9	10

I do not believe consequences will be tied to performance.

I am not certain consequences will be tied to performance.

I know for a fact that consequences will be tied to my performance.

COMMITMENT: How dedicated am I to perform this task well?

0	1	2	3	4	5	6	7	8	9	10

I have no desire to perform this task.

I am not sure how much I want to do this task.

I am totally committed to successfully completing this task.

(continued)

TOPS Rating Scales (continued)

COMMUNICATION: How well is information communicated in this organization?

0	1	2	3	4	5	6	7	8	9	10

| Information is not shared. | | | | I sometimes don't get all the information I require to do my job. | | | | Information is clearly communicated and shared. | | |

CHALLENGE: How hard or easy is it for me to successfully complete my job?

0	1	2	3	4	5	6	7	8	9	10

| The job is very easy and does not provide much of a challenge for me. | | | | The job provides a moderate challenge for me, but it is not very difficult. | | | | The job is very challenging and it motivates me to be successful. | | |

CONFLICT: What unresolved emotional or interpersonal issues exist?

0	1	2	3	4	5	6	7	8	9	10

| There are no conflicts in my life. | | | | There is some stress and conflict in my life that I must resolve. | | | | There is too much stress and too many conflicts in my life. | | |

CULTURE: How do the beliefs and values of the organization meet my desires?

0	1	2	3	4	5	6	7	8	9	10

| The organization's beliefs and values do not match my own. | | | | The organization's beliefs and values somewhat match my own. | | | | The organization's beliefs and values completely match my own. | | |

(continued)

TOPS Rating Scales (concluded)

CONTROL: How much perceived choice or control do I have while performing?

0	1	2	3	4	5	6	7	8	9	10

I feel I have little or no control over my performance.

I have some control and/or choice while performing.

I have complete control over my performance and its consequences.

CONCENTRATION: How well do I concentrate or focus my attention on a performance?

0	1	2	3	4	5	6	7	8	9	10

I have a great deal of difficulty focusing my attention and concentrating.

I am capable of focusing my attention some of the time.

I always maintain my concentration and focus while performing.

Now plot the ratings to provide your performer with a visual representation of his or her motivational approach and profile for performance improvement.

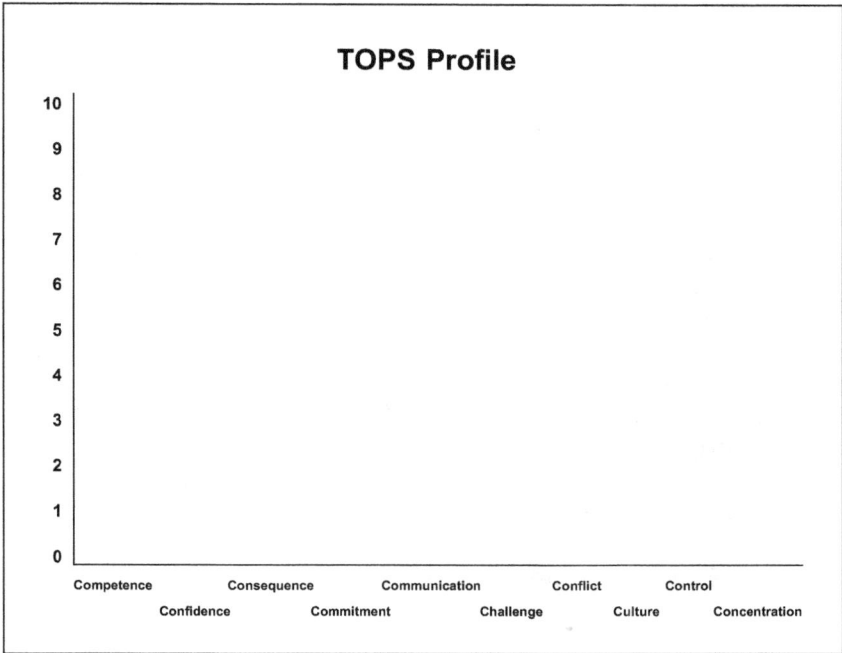

TOPS Profile

	Competence	Consequence	Communication	Conflict	Control
	Confidence	Commitment	Challenge	Culture	Concentration

(Y-axis: 0 through 10)

The Mastery Model

It is now time to introduce one final model for performance success, which focuses on what I call the **messy middle.** The messy middle refers to what goes on inside a performer before she actually performs. While we have been able to get at people's thoughts and attitudes through surveys, interviews, and even some physiological measurements, we seem to lack a job aid that helps us determine exactly what is going on in a performer's head and heart just prior to that performance. Well, that void has now been filled. Here is a job aid that will help you achieve performance mastery for any task you accomplish, given the appropriate amount of practice and effort. Since mastery of a task or skill is what we are all trying to achieve, I call this job aid the **MASTERY Model**. It is based on a proposal I made to the International Society for Performance Improvement (ISPI) to include a new "box" in their HPT model that focuses on assessing and analyzing the performer.[7]

Performer Analysis

When we analyze what makes a performance successful, we most often focus on the skills of the performer, the resources available to perform the task, and other systemic or organizational factors. The problem is there is minimal to no analysis of the internal states of the performer. We must spend more time working with and on the performer than on anything else if we want to enhance performance, improve performance, and guarantee performance. Consider the following example of a car and driver. You build the fastest, safest, most economical gas-mileage champion car ever. It is basically the perfect car. You test the car, and everything works perfectly. You find a driver and teach him how to "make the car sing." Now it is time for the test drive. Everything is ready and the conditions are perfect. But, for some reason, the driver is hesitant to drive. Whatever the reason, this driver is not going to perform no matter what you do. You have provided all the tools and resources for a great driving experience, but you still cannot get the driver to drive. What did you forget to do?

You forgot to "analyze" the driver to determine if he wants to drive this car. Does he believe he should drive this car? And you never asked him how he feels about driving the car? All these things and more impact the performance of the driver who is supposed to be driving the car. So even though all the systemic factors were considered, and the appropriate interventions were put into place, how come the personal motivational factors were left out or not considered?

Let's go through the performer analysis. For ease of description, I have broken down the analysis part into an acronym for **MASTERY**. I will define each of the seven aspects of MASTERY for the performer analysis along with each item's components. These components are recommended examples of what you should consider when assessing and analyzing a performer. The contents of this model are fluid and flexible, so you can add or delete information as you see fit.

Motivation. We should consider three types of motivation when we are analyzing a performer.

The first is approach/avoidance. This is also described as gain/loss or pleasure/pain. The concept is simply that people will either approach a task or avoid it, based on internal criteria that only they are aware of. We do know that more people will avoid an unpleasant situation (pain) than will approach an apparently pleasurable one (gain). This factor is also affected by incentives, rewards, and reinforcements, which we will discuss a little later in relation to another factor.

The second motivational issue is the motivational triad, or the big three. These refer to achievement, affiliation, and power. We all have a desire to achieve things, and this desire is stronger or weaker in each of us depending on how much risk we are willing to take, how important the result is to us, and how much we will benefit from the improvement. We also want to affiliate with other people because we are "social animals." Some people have a greater desire to be with people, while others have less of a desire. You must consider the social fabric of the performance situation and how the associated affiliation motivation can influence the performer. Witness the rapid growth of a variety of social networking sites on the Internet. That will give you all the information you require to know that affiliation is a powerful motivator. Finally, we all have a desire to control ourselves and our situations. This is one aspect of power motivation. It is also closely related to how much stress or pressure we feel when performing. A person who feels in control of the situation will be more motivated, feel more powerful, and be less stressed out during the performance.

The third motivational issue is the intrinsic/extrinsic continuum. People are more motivated to perform for intrinsic reasons than they are for extrinsic reasons. We must consider how much the person really wants to perform a task (intrinsic motivation) or how much of that performance motivation is based on the possible reward or payoff (extrinsic motivation).

This brings us to the question of how to measure a person's motivation in general, and performance-related motivation in particular. There are many ways you can do this, including tests, interviews, and observations. I have found that simply asking a person how motivated they are to perform the task and then delving into the reasons through a more facilitative questioning process usually uncover the roots and reasons of their motivation. You can also develop your own motivation rating scale (it does not necessarily have to be totally scientific or research validated to be effective) to help you and the performer get at motivation levels. You can also refer back to the Talent Optimization Performance System (TOPS) for a motivational "assessment tool" you can use.

Attributions. Attributions are the reasons people give for the results of their performances. Attributions can be internal or external, and they have an effect on future motivation and associated performances. For example, if a person attributes a performance decrement to a lack of ability, it is considered an internal attribution. Similarly, if a great performance is attributed to a high level of ability, that is also an internal attribution. If they attribute their performance results to a lack of effort or an increased effort, that is considered an external attribution. Both internal and external attributions have an effect on subsequent performances. You want the person to attribute a successful performance to things like ability, positive effort, and an understanding of how the task should have been performed. You also want them to attribute a poor performance to things like a lack of effort (which they can change for a future performance) rather than a lack of ability (which will negatively impact their confidence on future performances).

Because attributions can be made to a variety of things, you have to ask the performer what his or her reasons are for achieving the current or previous results. Once you have these answers, you may have to help the performer re-align attributions or even take them through what is called an attribution retraining process. The goal here is to make sure that successes are attributed more to internal factors, and failures are attributed more to external factors. This approach will positively impact the performer in future situations.

Self-confidence. Top performers are highly self-confident. People who do well on a task believe they will do well again and again. This is what we mean by a high level of self-confidence. Quite often, confidence is the major factor in performance results, especially in winning and losing streaks. People who are confident more often than not perform at a higher level because they believe in themselves and their ability to achieve. Self-confidence is also closely related to self-esteem. When we work with people to increase their self-esteem, we usually see a positive result in their related performances. People who feel good about themselves do better than people who are down on themselves. There is no denying the effect this has on a person or a performance. Just look at the way people who are self-confident carry themselves. They sit and stand taller; they walk more assuredly; and they speak with confidence. They are willing to tackle a task because they honestly believe they will succeed. In fact, they sometimes are even willing to take on more complicated or difficult tasks because their confidence is so high.

The implications for performance improvement are obvious. When you find a performance gap, ask the performer if they believe they are capable of successfully completing the task. It may not be a resource, skill, or process problem at all. It may simply be a belief problem. So if you can change the "confidence belief," you may easily get the performer to achieve at a higher level. Similarly, when you ask high performers to rate their confidence levels on a scale of 1 to 10, you will get a 9 or a 10 out of all of them.

Thoughts. Thoughts affect behavior, so it is imperative that you know what a performer is thinking relative to a given task. Without going into an entire textbook on cognitive psychology, suffice it to say that what a person thinks affects what she does and how she does it. Thoughts affect behavior. To help you in your performer analysis, here is what you must consider with regards to a performer's thoughts. I have created another mnemonic for you called **BEHAVE.**

Beliefs: The enabling or disabling thoughts we have about ourselves and our capabilities

Emotions: The positive and negative emotions that occur and that we control or that control us during a performance

Habits: The things we do almost automatically and without thinking

Attitudes: Our attitude determines our altitude, or how much we achieve; optimism is critical to success because it also feeds enabling beliefs

Values: Values that determine what is important to us and what we think, do, and produce

Experiences: People's past experiences that determine their future behaviors

Expectations. Expectations are our beliefs about our probabilities for success. They are intricately linked to our past performances and our beliefs about future performances. Quite often, the expectations a performer has about his potential for success will actually predetermine the performance result. Since you become and achieve what you think about most, performers who think about (expect) success succeed more often than not. Those who think about failure most of the time expect to perform poorly and they usually do. This is a form of the self-fulfilling prophecy and also goes back to the concept of enabling and disabling beliefs mentioned earlier.

Readiness. No one does anything well unless they are ready to perform. Sure, you can force someone to do something, but the result will most likely be less than optimal. Someone who is ready and prepared to perform usually possesses skills, knowledge, a high expectation of success, and past successful experiences; knows the reward that is available for effectively achieving the goal; and has a high degree of confidence.

The performer's state of readiness can be determined by observing pre-performance rituals, ongoing behaviors, interviewing the performer, testing the person's knowledge relative to the performance and expected outcomes, and reviewing practice routines. Readiness is a critical factor in performance improvement. Again, you can have all the tools and resources available, but if the person does not want to or is not ready to perform, either the performance will not occur or its results will be less than desirable.

YES. After the first six factors are taken into account, and they are all positive and aligned, then the performer decides to go forward. This **YES** decision only occurs after the performer goes through the entire process described above. Now, this trip through the mental processes of **MASTERY** may not even be done at the conscious level. Rest assured, though, that it will be done. It is like a person who wants to buy something. The seller has her agenda and wants to sell what she thinks the buyer wants. But the buyer must go through a series of mental processes related to motivation, decision making, and change before he makes the purchase. Similarly, every performer goes through a series of mental processes and decision-making stages before he says, "Yes, I will perform this task to the best of my ability." And every time this decision is made and the task is successfully completed, the reinforcement the performer receives enables him to run through this mastery process even faster next time.

One Last Thought

It really is not that difficult or frightening to be the person who guarantees performance improvement. Since results matter, and you are a seeker and an achiever of results, the desire and ability to guarantee performance improvement should be a challenge to you; one that you are willing to readily accept. With the tools and techniques described in this book, you have more than you require to achieve high levels of performance and guarantee performance improvement when someone's performance is not up to acceptable levels. Start with your Ideal

Vision—your Mega statement of how you will positively impact society. Keep all your other visions and beliefs aligned with the Mega or Ideal Vision. This will provide you with a tremendous guide throughout your journey to perfect performance. Next, know what is expected of you when you perform or what is expected of people you are coaching. Clearly communicate those expectations and identify the motivational factors that can help or hinder performance. Create the conditions for a performer to optimize his or her talents and strengths. Use the various job aids and tools in this last chapter to help you become one of the few people in the world who is willing to guarantee performance improvement. You will be more than satisfied at how well you and everyone around you is now performing. **I guarantee it.**

Endnotes

1. Kaufman, R., (2006). *Change, choices and consequences: A guide for Mega thinking and planning.* Amherst, MA: HRD Press.

2. See, for example, in addition to previous Kaufman works, Gerson, R. F., (2006). *Achieving high performance: A research-based practical approach.* Amherst, MA: HRD Press.

3. Gerson, R. F., & Gerson, R. G., (2006). *Positive performance improvement: A new paradigm for optimizing your workforce.* Palo Alto, CA: Davies Black Publishing.

4. The material contained in these two examples is taken verbatim from my previous book, *Achieving High Performance: A Research-based Practical Approach* (Amherst, MA: HRD Press).

5. The Talent Optimization Performance System (TOPS) was first introduced in a book by R. F. Gerson, & R. G. Gerson called *Positive Performance Improvement: A New Paradigm for Optimizing Your Workforce* (Palo Alto, CA: Davies-Black, 2006). It was then re-introduced in my book *Achieving High Performance: A Research-based Practical Approach* (Amherst, MA: HRD Press, 2006).

6. *Ibid.*

7. See Gerson, R. F., The missing link in HPT (January, 2006). *Performance Improvement 45* (1): 10–17.

About the Author

Richard F. Gerson, Ph.D., CPT, CMC

Richard Gerson, Ph.D., is president of **Gerson Goodson, Inc.**, a consulting and training firm specializing in elevating the performances of people, teams, and organizations by helping them identify and manage their thoughts, feelings, emotions, attitudes, and behaviors. He is also the owner of the **HEAD-coaching Institute**, which helps clients train their brains to become extraordinary performers.

Richard was one of the pioneers in the performance psychology field, having developed training programs and consulting services in this area since 1979. He is an expert in identifying behavioral and mental strategies that people use to perform at a high level and then developing training programs to both improve the performance of the exemplars and transfer those strategies to other performers. Richard's strength in helping others achieve high levels of performance and success lies in his abilities to coach and mentor people in such a way that they expand their comfort zones, stretch their limits, and turn the stresses of their lives into the successes of their lives. He uses a variety of techniques from sports and performance psychology, cognitive-behavioral psychology, and neurolinguistic psychology to accomplish these goals. He also helps salespeople, athletes, executives, and students **train their brains** to perform more effectively and successfully.

Richard has a Ph.D. in Sports Psychology from Florida State University. He has published 21 books and over 400 articles in journals, magazines, newspapers, and newsletters. He is a Certified Performance Technologist (the first in the Tampa Bay area), a Certified Management Consultant, a Certified Professional Marketing Consultant, and the holder of several other professional certifications. He was selected as the top marketing professional in Tampa Bay by the Sales and

Marketing Executives association and given a lifetime achievement award by the Tampa Bay chapter of the International Society for Performance Improvement, where he is also a past president and current board member. He has also just presented a workshop and a concurrent session at the upcoming ISPI conference.

Two of his books, *Winning the Inner Game of Selling and HEADcoaching: Mental Training for Peak Performance,* help salespeople and other professionals train their brains to achieve peak performance on demand. Several of his sales training programs, such as High Performance Selling, SPORT Selling, and Extraordinary Selling Power, have achieved sales increases for clients ranging from 10 percent to 500 percent.

Two of his most recent programs, **Positive CORE and The Talent Optimization Performance System (TOPS),** have helped individuals and organizations identify and remove roadblocks to performance improvement as well as enhance current performance strengths. These two approaches help clients virtually guarantee performance improvement in a variety of settings, including business, sports, academia and life in general. They also formed the basis for his newest book *Positive Performance Improvement: A New Paradigm for Optimizing Your Workforce,* which he co-authored with his wife, Robbie Goodson Gerson, and for another new book called *Achieving High Performance: A Research-based Practical Approach.*

He is a much sought-after speaker in the areas of sales success, performance psychology, performance improvement, motivation, marketing, and customer service. His use of sports and performance psychology applied to the business world, sports world, and academic environment helps people achieve their goals and objectives, motivate themselves to become peak performers, and continually increase their levels of skill to achieve measurable and sustainable performance improvements.

www.ingramcontent.com/pod-product-compliance
Lightning Source LLC
Chambersburg PA
CBHW071446200326
41518CB00028B/2038